Peter and Paul Stanley

The authors, twin brothers born in 1930, were brought up in Ilkeston, Derbyshire, in a predominantly coal-mining community. Their interest in athletics stems from the 1940s and particularly from the first post-war Olympic Games held in London in 1948.

During their working careers, Peter in the academic world and Paul as an accountant in the textile industry, their enthusiasm for athletics never waned and they have found great enjoyment in working together in researching Tom Hulatt's life and writing this book.

They hope to convey in it their admiration for Tom and all 'men and women of the track' whose efforts and dedication continue to inspire us all.

The First Four-Minute Mile

and

Tom Hulatt of Tibshelf

by

Peter and Paul Stanley

To Tom's sister, Ann

A CIP catalogue record of this book is available at the British Library

First published in 2003 by Descartes Publishing Limited

ISBN 0 9541718 1 0

Typeset by Mike Taylor; Cover by Karen Johnson; Editors: Liz Birchall and Sheila Harding. Printed and bound in Great Britain by Biddles Limited. Published by Descartes Publishing Limited, 83 Park Road, Peterborough, Cambridgeshire PE1 2TN

CONTENTS

Preface   3

Foreword by David Moorcroft   7

Introduction   9

Part I The First Four-Minute Mile
1. The AAA team   13   2. The OUAC team   16
3. Before the race   17   4. The venue   19
5. The race   20   6. After the race   26
7. The media   28   8. Ratification   34
9. Memorabilia   36   10. Landy and Vancouver   37

Part II   The Search
1. Beginnings   41   2. Tibshelf   44
3. Ann   47   4. Other sources   51
5. To Iffley Road   57

Part III W.T. Hulatt of Tibshelf
1. Early days   61   2. Before the four-minute mile 66
3. Oxford, 6 May 1954   74   4. After the four-minute mile   80
5. 1960 onwards   89   6. The press 'remembers'   94

Appendix I   World Record Times for One Mile: Comments and Observations
1. Through the 20th century   101   2. The future   104
3. The 'barrier'   108   4. An alternative presentation 109
5. Speeds and track dimensions 110   6. Miscellany   113
7. Figure A1   115   8. Figure A2   116

Appendix II A Record of Tom Hulatt's Races (1949-60)   117

Index   120

PREFACE

Retirement brings the opportunity to savour again the pleasures of one's youth. To us this meant (amongst other things) the re-reading of Roger Bannister's account of the epic mile event at the Iffley Road track in Oxford on 6 May 1954, in which he wrote himself indelibly into athletics history by breaking the four-minute mile 'barrier'. This marvellous achievement captivated the public mind in the same way that news of the first ascent of Everest by Edmund Hillary and Tenzing Norgay had done just before the Queen's Coronation, almost a year before. It was heroic; it was inspiring; we really were at long last well and truly clear of the dreary aftermath of the Second World War. The admiration for Bannister was boundless, and remains so.

The story never palls. Gusty, squally weather, a lull, the decision to have a go, a snatched opportunity; Brasher leading through the first lap, then the second and into the third, Chataway coming through and taking over, and Bannister breaking clear with 300 yards to go and finishing utterly exhausted in 3 min 59.4 sec. That same evening the news spread and the world applauded; it was truly wonderful.

We lingered over that fine picture of the start of the race, six young men launching themselves into four laps of supreme effort. We knew of Bannister, Brasher and Chataway, of course, and we found ourselves wondering – who were the other three? How had they come to be on the track in that event and how had they fared? Surprisingly quickly our enquiries focused in on one of the three, W.T. (Tom) Hulatt, described in some accounts as a miner from Derbyshire. Hailing ourselves from a Derbyshire mining town (or 'ex-mining' since all the pits are now closed) we found an easy affinity with the Tom we gradually discovered as we pursued our search. Tom died in 1990. His story is remarkable. This book is our attempt to tell that story as a tribute to a talented athlete and as a lasting record of his achievements. We look again at that windy May day in Oxford and try to see it as Tom might have done. We try to re-live his running career from the late 1940s, when his talents first showed themselves, through to the 1960s when he was still competing and coaching.

We hope too to convey something of the pleasure and growing sense of privilege we enjoyed in tracing and meeting the people who knew Tom and in building up our picture of him. We knew from the beginning that we would need patience, luck and help if we were to make any useful progress. Our patience, though sometimes taxed, didn't fail us and we had our share of

3

luck one way and another, but the indispensable ingredient, which underpinned whatever we were able to do, was the unstinted help of the numerous people we approached for information.

We record our thanks to:
J.G. De'Ath of Jesus College, Oxford, who first named the four-minute mile runners for us, for spending time with us at Iffley Road and making our visit there so enjoyable;
A. Keily of Derby and County Athletic Club, who, at the same time, recalled Tom Hulatt as one of the runners, and his brother J. Keily for letting us see and use papers relating to the Derbyshire Amateur Athletic Association (DAAA) and the Northern Counties Athletic Association (NCAA);
Paul Willcox, Hon. Sec. Achilles Club, who provided a photocopy of the official programme for the OUAC v AAA match at Oxford in May, 1954, and approved our use of the photocopy in preparing Figure 2 of this book;
Terry Watts of Alfreton, Derbyshire, who answered our 'request for information' notice in the Alfreton *Chad* newspaper, thereby enabling us to begin our enquiries, and his sister Joanne;
Christine Leeson of Tibshelf, for her help;
Cecil Hill of Tibshelf and his daughter Margaret for their reminiscences and for passing us on to Colin Croft;
Colin Croft of Tibshelf for introducing us to Miss Ann Hulatt, Tom's sister, and for telling us of Cyril Leason, his close friend;
the staff of Alfreton Library and Manchester Central Library for their patient assistance;
the staff of the *Derby Evening Telegraph* and *Derbyshire Times* for providing photocopies;
the staff of the Local Studies Libraries in Chesterfield, Derby and Sheffield for their help;
Rob Spedding for providing the May, 1994, issue of *Runner's World* and giving permission to quote therefrom;
Linda Hunter of the University Alumni Office, Oxford, and Frances Lawrence of the Development Office, University College, Oxford, for their help in establishing contact with C.J. Chataway, G.F. Dole, A.D. Gordon and T.N. Miller; and these four and R.G. Bannister and C.W. Brasher for responding to our enquiries;
Margaret Stocks of Selston, Notts, and her husband for their warm hospitality

and for sharing their recollections with us;

Anne Clarke of the National Centre for Athletic Literature (NCAL), Birmingham University, for her help;

Bill Adcocks (ex-Coventry Godiva Harriers), Barry Parker and Peter Wilkinson for helping us in our search and for their many helpful suggestions;

Alan Penn and Jean Wenger of the National Playing Fields Association (NPFA) for their patient help in establishing approved track dimensions;

George Livesey and Bryn Roberts for their internet searches and for their many helpful suggestions made after reading the draft;

Everard Hesketh of Tibshelf, Tom Hulatt's life-long friend, for his hospitality and reminiscences;

Eric Glover of Tibshelf for talking with us;

Stephanie Jackson for her patience and skills in transforming our manuscript into a top-quality typescript;

Denise Jackson for her help with the figures;

John Bates for providing information on railway matters;

Susan for her unfailing support and encouragement.

Most importantly, we wish to thank Miss Ann Hulatt of Tibshelf, Tom's sister, and Cyril Leason of Pilsley, his close friend. These two have treasured Tom's memory over the years and it has been a rare privilege to talk with them and to become their friends. They could not have been kinder or more helpful; without them this book would have amounted to very little indeed.

We also wish to acknowledge:

Airlife Publishing Ltd. for directing us to The Globe Pequot Press of Guilford, Connecticut, USA;

The Lyons Press, an imprint of The Globe Pequot Press Guilford, CT, for permission to quote from *The Four-Minute Mile*, copyright 2001 by Roger Bannister (Anna Clifford, the Subsidiary Rights Manager, was most helpful in our dealings with The Globe Pequot Press);

The Daily Mirror Group for permission to quote from their articles and those of *The Daily Sketch* and *The Daily Herald*;

NI Syndication Ltd. for permission to quote from articles in *The Times* and *The Sunday Times* and for providing Figure 1;

Express Newspapers for permission to quote from articles in *The Daily Express* and *The Sunday Express*;

The Daily Telegraph for permission to quote from various articles;

The Cambridge Alumni Magazine for permission to quote from the Lent Term 2002 issue;

The *Derby Evening Telegraph* for permission to reproduce Figure 6 and to use it on the cover, and to quote from various articles;

The *Derbyshire Times* for permission to quote from various articles;

The Croydon Advertiser Group for permission to reproduce Figure 7.

The Alfreton *Chad* newspaper for permission to reproduce Tom Hulatt's obituary.

The authors have gone to great lengths in their attempts to obtain permission to quote extracts and reproduce illustrations from various publications in this book. Occasionally they were not able to identify or locate the appropriate person or body, and sometimes, inadvertently, they may have assumed that such permission was unnecessary. Where material may have been included without formal permission, for these or any other reason, the authors offer their sincere apologies.

Peter and Paul Stanley, 2003

FOREWORD

I was born a year before Roger Bannister broke the four-minute mile barrier and I realised quite early on in my life that I had a love of running and in particular, the mile distance, which captured my imagination and shaped my ambitions.

Bannister's milestone is probably the most significant record in the history of athletics and the dream of breaking the four-minute barrier is still one that motivates middle distance runners the world over. I was one of those athletes who was driven by that challenge, but oh! what I would have given to be one of the privileged few who stood alongside Bannister on the start line at Iffley Road on 6th May, 1954.

Bannister's story and the roles that Chris Chataway and Chris Brasher played have been told many times, but few are aware of the story behind the other athletes who completed in that race. That is, until Peter and Paul Stanley took it upon themselves to write this fascinating book. Many people know that Chataway finished seond that day, and almost as many wrongly believe that Brasher finished third, but few know that a very special runner, from a mining community in Derbyshire, did, in fact take third place. That athlete was Tom Hulatt and it is his story that forms the basis of this excellent book.

In the past 50 years there have been huge changes to the equipment, facilities, support and the rewards available to athletes who compete at the highest level. However, the essential ingredients for success remain the same – talent, grit, determination and resilience are amongst those attributes and Tom had them in abundance. He was a club runner, turning out week after week all year round to give of his best and he was a classic example of the attitude and ability of the rich pool of talent that has underpinned Britain's athletic successes.

This book is well researched and a pleasure to read and it is particularly interesting to view Bannister's momentous day from a different angle. The main focus of sport is on today's performances, but the past is also of great significance and I am delighted to be associated with this tribute to a fine runner and to many cherished memories of one of the most significant eras in the history of our sport.

Dave Moorcroft

INTRODUCTION

*"We run, not because we think it is doing us good,
but because we enjoy it and cannot help ourselves."*
R.G. Bannister (First Four Minutes)

THE definitive account of the running of the first sub-four-minute mile has to be that given by Roger Bannister in his book *First Four Minutes* published by Putman's in 1955 one year after the event. (The price was 15 shillings (75p) and half of the royalties went to the AAA Coaching Fund.) The Sportsman's Book Club produced the book, unchanged, in 1956 and new editions from different publishers appeared in 1981 and 1994, the last, sadly, without illustrations and with the title changed to 'The Four-Minute Mile'. (The publishers thought, presumably, that this more explicit form would be helpful to a new generation.)

To anyone with a spark of interest in athletics the book is un-put-downable. It tells of the preparation, efforts and achievements of a young man, gifted both as an athlete and academically. It covers his running career from school in the mid-1940s, through Oxford, first as a Freshman then as an accomplished runner and President of the University Athletic Club, his role as 'assistant to the Commandant of the British team' in the 1948 Olympic Games at Wembley, his fourth place in the 1500m at the Helsinki Olympics in 1952, and finally his *annus mirabilis* of 1954, with his world record, his memorable victory over John Landy in the Empire and Commonwealth Games one-mile in Vancouver in August (the shots of him overtaking Landy as they entered the final straight must rank amongst the most dramatic moments in track athletics), and his 1500m victory at the European Games in Berne later that month. (Unaccountably, in the Introduction to the 1981 edition of his book, Bannister writes "After the four-minute mile ... I never competed again"!)

After 1954, with a characteristic single-mindedness, Bannister retired from athletics and embarked on an eminently successful career as a neurologist, and finally as Master of Pembroke College, Oxford.

The style of writing in Bannister's book is personal and introspective. It cannot be read without excitement and admiration, and as the centrepiece, the description of the four-minute mile stands out, unsurpassed. It took place very early in the season in the early evening of a dull blustery day, Thursday

6 May 1954, as an event in the annual match between teams representing the Oxford University Athletic Club (OUAC) and the Amateur Athletic Association (AAA) at the Iffley Road Athletic Ground in Oxford. The task facing Bannister required concentration of the very highest order and clearly his thinking would be locked entirely into the early running of his friends and AAA team-mates Chris Brasher, ex-Cambridge University, and Chris Chataway, ex-Oxford University, first class runners themselves with tremendous experience. (Brasher won the gold medal in the 3000m steeplechase at the Melbourne Olympics in 1956 and Chataway took the 5000m world record from the formidable Vladimir Kuts at the White City in the autumn of 1954.) The story unfolded around these three and, perhaps unsurprisingly, the other runners are not mentioned. In writing his account of the race Bannister had to re-live that intense effort of concentration which had controlled his physical effort and in that frame of mind, to all intents and purposes, only he, Brasher and Chataway were on the track. ("We had done it – the three of us", he writes.) It is also understandable that the media coverage of the race should have been targeted almost exclusively on these three runners. The other runners in the race appear to have slipped into a historical twilight. They are not the type who would have complained nor are we complaining on their behalf. We are not peddling the 'forgotten heroes' theme which has appeared a number of times in the press; this theme does credit to no one.

We were curious though, about the other runners. The well known photograph of the start of the race (Figure 1) shows six runners, two teams of three one supposes, Bannister, Brasher and Chataway making up the AAA team and the three others the OUAC team. But wait a minute, a closer look shows four AAA vests with the well known double hoop, and the broad dark blue Oxford bands on only two pairs of shorts. This seems a 4 versus 2 turnout. What has happened? Perhaps one of the Oxford team had to borrow AAA kit – surely not. Who were these people? We could not let matters rest; this had to be sorted out, and doing just that was the starting point of this story.

Where to begin? There must be archives and records in Oxford that would have all the information we wanted. A friend provided a telephone number for the Oxford University Sports Complex, where a young man said he didn't have the information to hand but would ring back. We rang him a week later. Yes, he'd found what we needed: the 'other runners' were A.D. Gordon (Magdalen College), G.F. Dole (University College – possibly an American) and W.T. Hulatt for the AAA. (The name Hulatt is spelt correctly here. Other printed versions include Hullatt, Hulett and Hullett. We have the authority of Miss Ann Hulatt in dismissing all versions but Hulatt.) A third Oxford man T.N. Miller was meant to run but didn't. We assumed that Hulatt was an agreed replacement for Miller and queried how an AAA man could be running for Oxford. The young man couldn't help on this and he referred us to John De'Ath, Fellow and Bursar of Jesus College, Oxford, from whom it seemed the information had been obtained. John De'Ath turned out to be a mine of information. He confirmed all the previous details and, regarding the fourth AAA man, his thinking was that this was agreed when it became clear that a sub-four-minute mile was a possibility. He thought that either Brasher or Chataway had been 'drawn in' as the fourth AAA team member making it a 4 versus 3 event. W.T. Hulatt was an original choice. On p.205 of the 1994 edition of his book Bannister writes:

"It was now less than three weeks to the Oxford University v. AAA race, the first opportunity of the year for us to attack the four-minute mile. Chris Chataway had decided to join Chris Brasher and myself in the AAA team."

Chris Chataway may have been 'drawn in' but his appearance in the match programme suggests that his inclusion was not a last minute decision. (There is no mention of W.T. Hulatt or the Oxford runners here or elsewhere in the book.) John De'Ath added that T.N Miller was the third member of the Oxford team but while his name appeared in the programme he didn't run. So there were seven names altogether in the programme event. The programme! "Do you have a copy?" "No, but my friend Paul Willcox has." What a find! The programme itself would resolve all our queries beyond any shadow of doubt.

Luck was with us. Paul Willcox was the Honorary Secretary of the Achilles Club and yes, he did have an original match programme (and a framed one at home!) and yes, he would let us have a photocopy. Sure enough within days a photocopy arrived. The real thing (Figure 2)! Event 9 read:

6.00 pm EVENT 9. ONE MILE

15. G.F. DOLE (Univ)　　　　　　**41. R.G. BANNISTER (Achilles)**
16. A.D. GORDON (Magdalen)　　**42. C.J. CHATAWAY (Achilles)**
58. T.N. MILLER (Univ)　　　　　　**43. W.T. HULATT (Alfreton)**
　　　　　　　　　　　　　　　　　　　44. C.W. BRASHER (Achilles)

At the same time, one of us (Paul) had pursued an entirely different line. He had made contact and become a friend of Arthur Keily, a very well known member of the Derby and County Athletic Club, with a longstanding record of success as a distance runner at local, national and international levels. He has produced a number of booklets on his running career. He was born in 1921 in Derby. Amongst his running achievements are: his three Marathon successes in 1954 (the Northern Counties Championship in 2 hr 30 min 45 sec, the All Ireland Championship in 2 hr 35 min 33 sec, and a Marathon in Liverpool in 2 hr 30 min 28 sec); his 25th place in 2 hr 27 min 0 sec in the Rome Olympic Marathon in 1960, having led the field over the early stages of the race; and his numerous titles and awards in the 1990s as a 70-plus-year-old Veteran. Paul asked if he knew who the other runners were in the first four-minute mile. The immediate reply, almost as if it were common knowledge, was "Oh yes, there was Tom Hulatt from Alfreton. He's dead now but he worked on the railway." (Arthur Keily himself had been a blacksmith's apprentice in the Derby Locomotive Works.) "He was a good runner but he wouldn't come to Derby to train. I beat him once – fancy a Marathon man beating a miler."

And so we found ourselves with all the Iffley Road runners identified. We might well have settled for that, our curiosity satisfied and our mini-project finished; it had barely begun! What fidgeted away in our minds persistently, like a stone in the shoe, was the name W.T. Hulatt (Alfreton). We knew something of the backgrounds of Bannister, Brasher and Chataway, they'd become prominent figures in their different ways, and we could imagine those of the Oxford runners Dole and Gordon. We also knew Alfreton, a small unsung town in Derbyshire straddling the (then) main Derby-Chesterfield road. Oxford offered dreaming spires and 'gilded youth'; Alfreton offered coal mining. Here was one of its sons in what turned out to be a milestone event in athletics. Who was W.T. Hulatt (Alfreton) and how had he come to be chosen as a member of the AAA team? Finding answers to these questions gave us pleasure and rewards we could not possibly have anticipated.

PART I

THE FIRST FOUR-MINUTE MILE

1. The AAA Team
2. The OUAC Team
3. Before the race
4. The venue
5. The race
6. After the race
7. The media
8. Ratification
9. Memorabilia
10. Landy and Vancouver

THE FIRST FOUR-MINUTE MILE

"... one record is only the prelude to another ..."
Athletics Correspondent, The Times, 7 May 1954

1. The AAA team

One can well imagine the buzz in athletics circles as the 1954 season approached. Would this be the year of the first sub-four-minute mile? Who would it be? Where would it be? There was no argument about the principal contenders – Santee, Landy and Bannister. Wes Santee, an American, had recorded a mile time of 4 min 2.4 sec early in 1953. Santee was beatable – he lost the Emsley Carr Mile in August 1953 to Gordon Pirie – but he was clearly someone to be reckoned with. (In fact, one month after Bannister's record run he produced a 4 min 0.6 sec time and a week after that 4 min 0.7 sec. Unfortunately he was suspended from competitive running in 1956 for infringement of the amateur rules.) John Landy was from Australia where, of course, the main running season coincides with our winter. In December 1952 he had run a 4 min 2.1 sec mile and a year later in a mile on the loose dirt track of Melbourne's Olympic Park he ran 4 min 2.0 sec. As if that were not fore-warning enough, in January, February and April of 1954, before the UK track season was under way, he was timed at 4 min 2.3 sec, 4 min 2.6 sec and, again, 4 min 2.6 sec. The antipodean challenge could not have been clearer.

The opportunity offered by the annual OUAC v. AAA match on 6 May must have been recognised well before the event and the selection of Bannister, Brasher and Chataway for the AAA team would have required no great debate. They were long-standing friends. They had trained together. Bannister writes:

"In my hardest training Chris Brasher was with me, and he made the task very much lighter. On Friday evenings he took me along to Chelsea Barracks where his coach, Franz Stampfl, held a training session. At weekends Chris Chataway would join us, and in this friendly atmosphere the very severe training we did became most enjoyable."

They were all top-flight athletes. A major joint success had been the achievement of a new British National record of 15 min 49.6 sec in a 4 x 1500m relay in May 1953. (They ran as Achilles Club members; the fourth man was D.C. Law.) They seemed a ready-made team. Even so, it appears that their choice was not straightforward. Bannister recalls (see Introduction) that, with less than three weeks to go, "Chris Chataway had decided to join Chris Brasher and myself in the AAA team". This suggests that Chataway was 'roped in' and that Bannister and Brasher were the original nucleus. However, writing in the *Daily Telegraph* of 3 August 1995, Donald Trelford noted that:

"Christopher Brasher, who paced the others, was not selected for the event but persuaded the organisers to include him for the record bid."

Just who joined whom in the threesome remains unclear, but a more intriguing question is how W.T. Hulatt came to be brought in.

There are in fact two questions – why an AAA team of four and why Tom Hulatt? ('Team' here, of course, means the one-mile runners and not the full AAA turnout.) The usual team would be two or three. There were sixteen events altogether in the match programme including the 4 x 110 yards relay. Leaving aside the relay, in all but three of the events both sides fielded two competitors. In the two-miles there were three from each side; in the 120 yards hurdles there was an extra AAA entrant; and in the one-mile there were three Oxford and four AAA runners. The Bannister/Brasher/Chataway threesome was tailor-made for the task in hand. Why add to it? It has been suggested that the principal factor here was the understandable anxiety on the part of the AAA selectors to offset any possible charges of pace-making. Whilst nowadays it is a commonplace feature of record-making, in those days pace-making, that is the inclusion of people in a race for the purpose of assisting one particular runner to win, was completely unacceptable. There was often a fine line to be drawn between pace-making and acceptable teamwork in which members of a team pooled their talents and settled their tactics so as to ensure victory for the team. Be that as it may, anything that smacked of deliberate pace-making was anathema to ratifying organisations.

Bannister himself had run foul of this bogey when he ran in a special invitation mile race in the Surrey Schools sports meeting at Motspur Park in June 1953, his first turn-out after a pulled muscle. Brasher was also in the race. He held back for his first 1¹/₂ laps until Bannister, then well into his third lap, came up behind him; from thereon he led Bannister through to the finish, shouting encouragement to him over his shoulder the while. The recorded time was 4 min 2.0 sec. The race was a fiasco. *The Times* correspondent wrote:

> **"The profound secrecy with which the project was planned and carried out ... prevented all but a favoured few from being able to give an eye-witness account ...**
>
> **"Nor is one quite sure about the motive behind the secrecy. Some will think Bannister, at the start at any rate, was concerned mainly with testing more or less in private the muscle he pulled a few weeks ago. Or he may have been seriously intent upon the exceptional time he in fact achieved without any preliminary speculation on the subject. Or, if one dare suggest such a thing, he may even have had the four-minute mile itself in mind. Doubtless also there was the knowledge that almost simultaneously W. Santee, the American who recently startled the world by doing the distance in 4 min 2.4 sec, was having another go ..."**

The time was not ratified as a record, much to Bannister's relief in the circumstances, and he stonewalled determinedly with a "No comment" against a barrage of questions from journalists. (In the *Daily Telegraph* of 7 May 1954, Jack Crump refers somewhat dismissively to a "technical non-compliance with the required conditions"!) Interestingly, his time of 4 min 3.6 sec achieved at the 1953 OUAC v. AAA match in May, with Chataway having "agreed to run as hard as he could for the first ³/₄ mile", was ratified as a British All-comers' and British National record. (Oddly enough, the two were in opposing sides for this match, Bannister in the AAA team and Chataway still with the OUAC.)

The suggestion referred to above is that the AAA selectors wanted to include in the team a runner patently unrelated to the threesome. (The possibility of not including one of the three could not be contemplated.) Where better to look than the Northern Counties? The (then) current Northern Counties One-Mile Champion was Tom Hulatt! This line of thinking does offer some kind of rationale for his inclusion in the team; we have not been able to find a better one. There were certainly milers around with better times than Tom's, but it was early in the season, current form outside the university world had hardly been established and the choice of the 1953 Northern Counties Champion avoided endless agonising and debate. We presume that a formal written invitation was sent to Tom but no record of this has survived. None of the other AAA team members has been able to shed light on his selection.

2. The OUAC team

This team would have been chosen by the club officers – notably the President and Honorary Secretary. Thanks to the help of the Oxford University Alumni Office and the Development Office, University College, we have been able to make contact with each of the three team-members named in the programme, G.F. Dole (Univ.), A.D. Gordon (Magdalen) and T.N. Miller (Univ.). G. (George) F. Dole was an American student in Oxford studying Hebrew in preparation for his ordination as a Baptist minister. He was in his early twenties and had established his claim to a place in the team by winning the one-mile race in the Oxford v. Cambridge match at the White City Stadium, London, earlier in the year. His enthusiasm for running and his energy can be judged from the fact that the Iffley Road mile was the first of five races for him in three days!

A. (Alan) D. Gordon had completed his National Service and had arrived in Oxford in 1953 to read history. He had shown his talents as a runner whilst in the Army, setting a new Egyptian Army mile record, and he quickly confirmed his standing once at the University with a new Freshman's mile record and third place in the 1954 Oxford v. Cambridge match. Like Tom Hulatt he was from Derbyshire; his hometown was Bolsover, near Chesterfield, some six miles from Tom's home in Tibshelf. Their paths crossed in 1954 just before the Iffley Road match when they both ran in a one-mile race in Manchester, and after then their names often appeared together, usually in different events, in various match programmes. At the time of the four-minute mile Gordon was a member of the Chesterfield Harriers and Athletic Club where Tom competed with great success in the late 1950s and where eventually he took up coaching.

T.N. (Nigel) Miller was the non-competing team member! In 1954 he was a 20-year-old medical student at Oxford with successes over a good range of middle distances. He went along to the evening match to spectate and there in the programme he saw his own name! No one had told him he was in the team. The OUAC Secretary thought that the President had told him; the President thought that the Secretary had told him. He had no kit with him and the chance of borrowing a pair of well-fitting spikes was zero. He had no choice, unfortunately, but to stay out of a piece of history.

3. Before the race

There was certainly a whiff in the air that something might be on. Bannister's capabilities and aspirations were of course no secret and insiders knew of his very demanding training schedule through the winter. They might also have noted times of 3 min 0 sec for a 3/4 mile at Motspur Park, and 2 min 59.9 sec for the same distance and 1 min 54 sec for a 1/2 mile on a Paddington track – all in the last week of April.

Murmurings appeared on Tuesday 4 May when *The Times* gave the Oxford team details for the match and surmised that something special might be afoot in the mile. The Oxford runners were named as G.F. Dole (University) and A.D. Gordon (Magdalen); there was no mention of T.N. Miller, the third Oxford team member.

On the day of the race the Athletics Correspondent of *The Times* noted, "The whole world now seems to be set upon the elusive four-minute mile". He mentioned Landy and Santee and reminded readers of the burgeoning talents of a young New Zealander, Murray Halberg, with a recent mile time of 4 min 4.4 sec. He wrote also about a virtually unknown Scot, A. Breckinridge, studying at Villanova University in the States, who "to the general amazement" had produced a 4 min 6.3 sec mile on a boarded track to beat the renowned Mal Whitfield, double Olympic gold medallist in the 800m. (This run ousted Gordon Pirie from third place in the UK all-time mile list behind Bannister and Sidney Wooderson.) Notwithstanding this high-level competition, the correspondent declared:

" ... the belief that if any British miler in the next year or so was to achieve the four-minute mile, Bannister was the man. Today he will have Chataway on the same side, in an AAA team which includes a number of men in the running for places at the Empire Games and European Championships."

The Daily Telegraph of 4 May also gave the Oxford team information. There was no speculation at all about a possible record and, again, no mention of Miller. The 6 May issue carried an article by a Special Correspondent entitled "Fast mile likely tonight":

> **"Tonight's match at Iffley Road between Oxford University and the AAA will begin in an atmosphere of subdued expectancy. In last year's match R.G. Bannister, helped by his Oxford opponent C.J. Chataway, won the mile in the British Record time of 4 min 3.6 sec.**
>
> **Bannister and Chataway again run in the mile but this time as AAA team-mates against their old University. Nothing that either has said would justify the strong belief that they intend to try for a really fast time, but they have run fast times together in training and it is probable that Bannister, sensitive to pre-race publicity, will make a big effort to improve on his present record."**

(The record referred to was presumably the British All-comers and British National record of 4 min 3.6 sec, set at the 1953 match.)

Perhaps typically, the *Daily Express* found a new angle on the race. In a short article on 6 May ("U.S. star can help Roger") its Bob Pennington wrote:

> **"Roger Bannister, Britain's mightiest miler, can be the first man to run a mile in four minutes at Oxford today.**
>
> **"But he must have the cooperation of his AAA team-mates Chris Chataway and Chris Brasher ... and the consent of his Oxford University rival poker-faced American George Dole.**
>
> **"Dole's dilemma is whether to do what is best for his team, or forget that the event is part of a match, and help Bannister to that fabulous mile.**
>
> **"And what is the result of an AAA-University match compared with the four-minute mile?**
>
> **"Slim, fair-haired Dole, winner of the inter-varsity mile last March, can make Bannister race the first two laps well within two minutes. Times of 1.58 or 1.59 would be within their powers.**
>
> **"Dole can aid Chataway to complete the vital third lap in three minutes, leaving Bannister to pile on the pace for the last lap.**

"Yes, it can be done. Bannister and Chataway proved it at Motspur Park a fortnight ago, completing three laps in three minutes watched by Bill Nankeville and coach Geoff Dyson.

"Much depends on getting Bannister to the bell within three minutes. His superb finishing burst can be relied on for the rest."

One can but sympathise with Dole in his dilemma! The time details are about right – as they had to be, of course – and Chataway did take over for most of the third lap, but the misreading of Dole's role in the race must take the prize as a piece of inventive journalism.

4. The venue

The Iffley Road Athletic Ground is an easy 15 min walk (or an easier 5 min bike ride) from the centre of Oxford, overlooked – sentinel-like – by the stocky crenellated tower of St John's Church. The facilities – hardly lavish – were housed in the mock-Tudor clubhouse, familiar from many photographs of the day but long since replaced. There was a small covered stand for spectators towards the finishing end of the home straight. The ground had been extensively remodelled in the late 1940s, largely as a result of the efforts of Bannister himself, then President of the OUAC. The work involved the replacement of the archaic 1/3 mile circuit (like the Cambridge track at Fenner's at the time) by a 440-yard six-lane track conforming in all respects with international specifications. The new track was opened in 1950. (The central area was, and still is, used as a soccer pitch for two terms of the academic year.)

The construction of a new track of an international standard was a highly specialised operation involving excavation, marking-out, levelling, the provision of drainage and the laying of the track itself. (An authoritative text on the subject from the 1950s is *The Planning, Construction and Maintenance of Playing Fields* by Percy White Smith, Chief Technical Adviser to the National Playing Fields Association.) The track consisted of consolidated layers of coarse and fine boiler ash (clinker) with a layer of fine ash blended with clay or marl and sand. The actual surface was a one-inch thick layer of blended ash, clay and sand in specified proportions, consolidated by rolling. This was the 'cinder track' which preceded modern all-weather surfaces. Maintenance consisted of stiff brushing or light raking and then a rolling to ensure a clean, well compacted surface. A good track, well maintained, would stay in use for many years before major resurfacing became necessary.

5. The race

It was an inclement evening and, with examinations looming for many students, the match attracted only a sprinkling of spectators. Estimates of numbers vary from "fewer than 1000" (unattributed cutting), through "nearly 2000" (Jack Crump, *Daily Telegraph*, 7 May 1954) to "the crowd of 3000" (Roy Moor, *News Chronicle*, 7 May 1954). As a forty-year-old afterthought *The Sunday Times* of 1 May 1994 gives an attendance of 1200. Bannister doesn't venture a figure in his book but in the same issue of *The Sunday Times* he is quoted as saying:

> **"... if everyone who said they watched the race that night actually had, they wouldn't have fitted in Wembley, let alone Iffley Road."**

Inside the track and hovering around the finishing line there was a cluster of officials, principally of course the starter and timekeepers, and their entourage. There is a detailed listing on the front page of the match programme. People not listed, but important nevertheless, included Jack Crump, Norris McWhirter and Franz Stampfl. Jack Crump, Secretary of the British Amateur Athletic Board, was a prominent sports administrator of the period. Quite in what capacity he was there is not known (L.R. Truelove was the AAA Team Manager) but a very well informed report appeared under his name in the *Daily Telegraph* the day after the race. Doubtless too his experience and knowledge would have been called upon when the ratification paperwork was completed and launched on its way. Norris McWhirter, an ex OUAC athlete, was the 'announcer'. His name did appear in the match programme but on the last page, as a member of the AAA team in the 4 x 110 yard relay, the last event of the meeting timed at 7.05 pm; the AAA team won in 43.7 sec. Norris McWhirter and his twin brother Ross (tragically shot at his home by the IRA in 1975) were well-known journalists who produced the first *Guinness Book of Records*. They were particularly close to Roger Bannister who wrote:

> **"The energy of the twins, Norris and Ross McWhirter, was boundless. For them nothing was too much trouble, and they accepted any challenge joyfully. After running together in Oxford as sprinters they carried their partnership into journalism, keeping me posted of the performance of my overseas rivals. They often drove me to athletics meetings, so that I arrived with no fuss, never a minute too soon or too late. Sometimes I was not sure whether it was Norris or Ross who**

held the watch or drove the car, but I know that either could be relied upon."

Franz Stampfl, an athlete in his young days and latterly a coach, was Austrian by birth. He had come to the UK in the 1930s as a refugee from the Nazi regime and had been interned as an alien for a period during the Second World War. By the 1950s, however, he had established himself as a highly respected coach and athletics guru. He had been at the Chelsea Barracks training sessions that Bannister had shared with Brasher and Chataway and from Brasher's recollections (*Sunday Times*, 1 May 1994) it seems that he played a part in formulating the overall tactics for the four-minute mile. Bannister never used a coach, as normally understood, but he had much respect for Stampfl's views and advice. Quite by chance the two of them travelled to Oxford from London in the same railway carriage and Bannister found much benefit in Stampfl's encouragement. He writes "in my mind I had settled this as the day when, with every ounce of strength I possessed, I would attempt to run the four-minute mile." Yet he also writes "I had almost decided when I entered the carriage at Paddington that unless the wind dropped soon I would postpone the attempt." His dilemma was clear. Stampfl thought that he was capable of running the mile in 3 min 56 sec and stressed that the 'will to win' was all-important. He mentioned too that the future might not hold many more such chances. The knowledge that the opportunity ahead might be unique was uppermost in Bannister's mind as the train pulled into Oxford station.

Six o'clock approached, the hurdles from the previous event were cleared away and the six runners assembled on the track. The decision whether or not to go for the record was Bannister's alone – it had to be. As they lined up for the start he noticed that the St George's flag on St John's Church tower, which earlier had stood out from the flagpole, was fluttering gently. That clinched it. The wind had eased. The attempt was on.

Bannister's account of the race itself takes up just two pages of his book. After a false start Brasher led into the first bend with Bannister "feeling tremendously full of running" close behind. Brasher ignored a "Faster!" shout from Bannister and held the pace at what he knew to be right for the job in hand. However, Bannister's anxiety remained with him through to the middle of the second lap when he heard Franz Stampfl's "Relax". He need not have worried; the half-mile time of 1 min 58 sec was ideal. After the next bend Chataway took over from Brasher and brought them through the psychologically demanding third lap in 3 min 0.7 sec (sic). Chataway continued to lead round the bend then, Bannister writes:

> "... I pounced past him at the beginning of the back straight, three hundred yards from the finish.
>
> "I had a moment of mixed joy and anguish, when my mind took over. It raced well ahead of my body and drew my body compellingly forward. I felt that the moment of a lifetime had come. There was no pain, only a great unity of movement and aim. The world seemed to stand still, or did not exist. The only reality was the next two hundred yards of track under my feet. The tape meant finality – extinction perhaps...I had now turned the last bend and there were only fifty yards more.
>
> "My body had long since exhausted all its energy, but it went on running just the same. The physical overdraft came only from greater willpower ... With five yards to go the tape seemed almost to recede. Would I ever reach it? Those last few seconds seemed never-ending...I leapt at the tape like a man taking his last spring to save himself from the chasm that threatens to engulf him.
>
> "My effort was over and I collapsed almost unconscious, with an arm on either side of me. It was only then that real pain overtook me. I felt like an exploded flashlight with no will to live ..."

Very shortly afterwards, as Bannister recovered, Norris McWhirter's tantalisingly formal announcement came over:

> "Ladies and gentlemen, here is the result of event number nine, the one mile: First, number 41, R.G. Bannister of the Amateur Athletic Association and formerly of Exeter and Merton Colleges, with a time which is a new meeting and track record and which, subject to ratification, will be a new English Native, British National, British All-comers', European, British Empire and World record. The time is 3 min (a wild outburst of cheering) 59.4 sec."

The complete result as recorded by the IAAF (then the International Amateur Athletic Federation, now the International Association of Athletics Federations) in *Progression of World Best Performances and Official IAAF World Records* compiled in 1995 by Ekkehard zur Megede was:

1. **Roger Bannister**   **3 min 59.4 sec**
   (all three watches recorded 3 min 59.4 sec)
2. **Chris Chataway**   **4 min 7.4 sec***
3. **William Hulatt**   **4 min 16.0 sec**
4. **Alan Gordon**
5. **G.F. Dole (USA)**
6. **Chris Brasher**

*Several accounts give Chataway's time as 4 min 7.2 sec. The time given is that recorded by the IAAF.

Bannister's time at the 1500m mark, some 119.6 yards short of the one-mile finishing line, was taken as 3 min 43 sec, a time equal to the (then) world record for that distance held jointly by Lennart Strand and Gundar Hägg of Sweden and the German Werner Lueg. Unfortunately this single recorded time could not be submitted for ratification because several independent timings are essential for that purpose. It should be noted also that, contrary to at least one national newspaper, this 1500m timing could not have been taken by Franz Stampfl since he is shown in many press photographs as supporting Bannister moments after he crossed the finishing line.

The accepted lap timings and the more speculative 220 yards split times (as given in the *Guardian Journal* of 7 May 1954) were:

Distance (yards)	Time (min: sec)	220 yards interval time (sec)	Lap time (sec)
220	28.7	28.7	
440	57.5	28.8	57.5
660	1:27.5	30.0	
880	1:58.2	30.7	60.7
1100	2:29.6	31.4	
1320	3:00.5	30.9	62.3
1540	3:30.4	29.9	
1760	3:59.4	29.0	58.9

(It is just possible that T.N. Miller obtained some of the half-lap timings.) Not all accounts give the same lap times and it seems possible that insufficient distinction has been made between the times for the leading runner and those for Bannister himself. Jack Crump (*Daily Telegraph*, 7 May 1954) is quite specific in giving the above figures as Bannister's lap times but *The Times* (7 May 1954) gives lap times differing by up to 0.2 sec, and values derived from Bannister's own account are 57.5 sec, 60.5 sec, 62.7 sec and 58.7 sec; in the *Runner's World* of May 1994 they appear as tabulated above. The first lap, fuelled in part by nervous energy, was the fastest and the third the slowest. The difference of 4.8 sec in these times may have surprised the runners in retrospect, but the three-lap time was almost exactly what they had aimed for.

No times are given for the last three runners. This is not unusual and in this case in particular the timekeepers might well have been distracted by the surge of well-intentioned people inside the track coming forward to help or congratulate Bannister. (Tom Hulatt – see Part III – has recalled that when he reached the finishing line "The track was in a turmoil with crowds of people swarming to congratulate Roger.") G.F. Dole, however, has provided an interesting item of information. In his e-mail to the authors of 4 April 2001 he writes:

"I recently located the letter I wrote home shortly after the race (May tenth) in which I told my parents that I had finished last in about 4 min 25 sec."

Alan Gordon recalls that "he (Tom Hulatt) beat me in the run-in for third place" and Tom Hulatt himself has described his placing as "a comfortable third".

Pointlessly but perhaps inevitably, it is asked how far behind were the other runners when Bannister broke the tape? If one assumes that each runner completed the race at a constant average speed then it is readily shown that Chataway would have been about 57 yards behind Bannister, Hulatt about twice as far behind and Dole, coincidentally, about three times as far. But these figures are simplistic. Speeds might well have changed as the race drew to an end. It might be thought, for example, that Chataway, his task accomplished, would have slowed down; however, he couldn't have lost much speed in the latter stages since his time was a personal best for him at the time. For Hulatt too, the challenge from Gordon would have served as a strong incentive to 'find something extra' for the closing stages. Dole might have slowed down. The figures given are the best that can be done; they are not accurate but they give an indication of the distances between the runners at the finish.

Chris Brasher, 'always a gallant and willing runner', played a crucial part in the final outcome of the race, but accounts of what became of him after Chataway took over the lead in the third lap differ. *The Times* wrote, "Brasher dropped back and, one fears, became forgotten though he had deserved well of all concerned". Other concurrent press reports are similarly non-committal. The *Daily Mirror* said that he "slowed to a walking pace", and the *Daily Sketch* that, having made his contribution, he "died out of the running". *The News Chronicle* went further, noting, "he (Chataway) set up such a killing rate that Brasher had to retire from the race". The *Daily Express* quoted Brasher as saying "I did not have a decent stride left". So, it might be thought that Brasher did not finish. However, the official IAAF record places him in sixth place and, in recent private correspondence, he also puts himself sixth. The *Runner's World* issue of May 1994 lists him as fourth (with Dole and Gordon "not finishing"!), as does Peter Matthews in *The Guinness Book of Athletics Facts and Feats* (1982). In the *Daily Telegraph* of 3 August 1995 Donald Trelford writes "some readers say he (Brasher) never finished the race, but he insists that he did!". The latest published word, as far as we are aware, comes from Brasher himself. In the Lent Term 2002 issue of *CAM*, the *Cambridge Alumni Magazine*, he recalls, "I was the pacemaker for the first two-and-a-half laps, but came in about fifth". There is no clear, simple way of reconciling these various reported placings, the recollections of Brasher and Dole, and the IAAF record. However there is no strong argument for questioning the IAAF record and it is suggested that this is accepted as authoritative.

As the race developed, spectators were lifted to a crescendo of excitement, barely touched by Bannister's all-to-evident state of absolute exhaustion as he crossed the finishing line. He was clearly on the point of collapse. The *Daily Sketch* reporter writes that "he was out on his feet for at least four minutes". Support came immediately from his friend Nicolas Stacey (a room-mate at the Helsinki Olympics), Franz Stampfl and the dependable Les Truelove, the AAA team manager. It is a tribute to Bannister's remarkable level of fitness that within minutes he had recovered from this parlous state and was up on his toes smiling, joining Brasher and Chataway to share the moment with them.

6. After the race

The race finished just after 6pm. The television programme *Sportsview*, from the Lime Grove Studios, London, started at 8.20 pm and, incredibly, Roger Bannister appeared live on this programme. Considering all that must have been packed into the intervening period, one cannot help but be amazed that this could have been possible. He had to recover. He then had to oblige the press photographers and reporters, and face a veritable barrage of congratulations from friends, officials and invading spectators before he could begin to make his way back to the changing room. (He would also need a moment to say hello to his parents who, unknown to him, had been spirited up from their home in Harrow-on-the-Hill to watch the race.) There would be no abatement en route – photographs, backslapping, autographs, jostling – and even inside the building this would continue. This was a momentous occasion and excitement was sky-high. One reporter writes "The amazing scenes of congratulation after the race went on for almost an hour."

He then had to find his clothes, as best he could, shower, dress and face the admiring crowd again. He managed to get away. He recounts, "as told to a *Daily Express* reporter", "I went off with friends to Vincent's Club at Oxford and had a pint of shandy." (Club membership comprises mainly sportsmen, many of them with 'a full Blue' for representing the University against Cambridge.) One might guess that even in these circumstances, it would be difficult to do justice to a pint shandy in less than 10-15 minutes. Then away to a car and off to London. The Oxford-London distance along the old A40 is given in the RAC handbook as 57 miles – perhaps up to $1\frac{1}{2}$ hours motoring in the late evening. Having arrived at Lime Grove, with perhaps a moment to collect himself, Bannister would be whisked off to the studio where he was congratulated and interviewed by Peter Dimmock, Head of Outside Broadcasts. He was relaxed and composed, showing not the least sign of rush or trouble. He is quoted as saying, "I think the four-minute mile has been over-rated ... the essence of athletics is racing against opponents rather than against the clock."

The detailed logistics of the transfer to Lime Grove are not altogether clear. The *Daily Herald* refers quite specifically to "a BBC car" and Bannister writes in his book "I was to meet the Chrises in London later and I travelled up by car for a television programme." However, one reporter writes "He travelled back to London last night in Chataway's car". Chris Brasher assures us (see later) that they used Chataway's car (a pre-war Austin 8) in London later that evening but it seems most probable that Bannister used independent transport for his journey. It cannot be supposed that the BBC acted spontaneously after the result of the race became known. Clearly, plans must have been laid well beforehand. Just who flagged the event to the BBC, and when, is not known.

Information from an internet search by our friend (and brother-in-law) Bryn Roberts further muddies the picture. The search produced the 'Personal Reminiscences' of a Kay Madan Mohan (née Broadley) who worked at the Lime Grove Studios in the 1950s as a 'vision mixer'. She writes:

> **"I was vision mixing a sports programme (*Sportsview*) the day Roger Bannister, Chris Chataway and Chris Brasher ran the under-four-minute mile. Paul Fox was in the control room and kept ringing up to find out if the race had been run, and when it had, all three participants came to Lime Grove to appear in the programme."**

However they may have travelled and whoever turned up at the Lime Grove Studios, and accepting that there were no competing television channels at the time, it is certain that the broadcast must have been seen as a huge scoop for the fledgling medium.

It is also certain that after the broadcast the three spent the night 'on the town' together in London. Bannister himself is noticeably reticent about their celebrations, devoting a single joyless sentence to them in his book – "We had an evening of celebration." More is forthcoming from the *Daily Express* and *Daily Sketch* of 7 May 1954. In the northern edition of the *Express* a small article headed "A little party", clinging to the bottom of the front page, read:

> **"Roger Bannister arrived at the Royal Court Theatre in Sloane Square as the audience was leaving last night. He strode through unrecognised and ran up a staircase to a club over the theatre.**
>
> **"He was joined at a table by a tall fair girl in an off-the-shoulder green gown.**
>
> **"At 12.50 this morning he said 'I feel like dancing until dawn and I may yet do.' He had finished a four-minute steak and several glasses of champagne."**

The *Daily Sketch* confirmed this tale of high living, adding that the three of them were there, with three girlfriends, and noting that there appeared an iced cake with the inscription 'Four-Minute Mile'.

Chris Brasher's account of the evening, which appeared in a *Sunday Times* article in 1994, leaves no doubt that they had a whale of a time and, in describing an encounter with a policeman at Piccadilly Circus in the small hours, confirms that Chris Chataway's car did actually make it to London.

The Press would be out in force on Friday 7 May, aiming particularly for Bannister. He managed to construct an escape route from his home through the garden and make his way back to Oxford for a "quiet day" with friends there. (*The Times* reported him as "resting quietly in London".) What course of restoration and recovery the Chrises took is not recorded.

7. The media
Clearly, by the day of the race, the word was around that something very, very special was in the offing. The national press was there in force with reporters and photographers; the BBC Television Newsreel crew was there and the ciné cameras of the British-Gaumont and Universal news teams. The outcome must have exceeded their wildest dreams. They had witnessed and recorded history in the making, absolutely unique and unrepeatable, a barrier broken once and for all time, and new vistas of challenge and achievement ahead.

The TV coverage of the event is still seen as a classical example of sports reporting. (The TV broadcasting of the Queen's Coronation in June 1953 was the single biggest factor in boosting television sales in the 1950s, but Bannister's mile and Chataway's 5000m victory over Vladimir Kuts in a flood-lit evening match between London and Moscow at the White City in October were hugely influential in persuading the die-hards of the unparalleled scope and potential of the new medium.) The film was shown on the evening of Friday 7 May. Writing in the *Daily Express* the following day, Robert Cannell reported:

> **"Roger Bannister ... did it all over again last night in TV's most exciting four minutes of film before an audience of six to seven millions ...**
>
> **"They (the two cameramen) produced brilliant, breathless pictures which had me clapping hands in excitement as Bannister hurled himself over the last few yards to the tape and the record ...**
>
> **"I rate this four-minute film the finest and most exciting piece of TV this year, and a fine technical achievement."**

The high quality of the ciné film is evident in a sample of frames published under the title 'The Miracle Mile' which highlights the front-running of first Brasher and then Chataway as the laps are reeled off. The first frame shows each of the six competitors just before the start, with the starter himself behind them, white-coated and pistol raised. (The runners are not correctly identified in the caption.) A minor oddity in the line-up is that Bannister, standing fourth from the inside of the track, is the only runner toeing the line with his right foot, the others lead off the left foot.

On Friday 7 May every national newspaper in the country carried the story, the tone varying from the dignified praise of the broadsheets to the rapturous acclaim of the popular press. The main story in *The Times* appeared in a single $2^{1}/_{2}$ inch wide column on p.8, with a small ($2^{1}/_{4}$ x 4 inch) picture of Bannister breaking the tape, headed "4-Minute Mile, Triumph of R.G. Bannister, Poor Conditions Overcome". (In the format of those days the whole of the front page of *The Times* was given to columns of notices and announcements.) In his opening paragraph, the Athletics Correspondent writes that "he (Bannister) finished weary but triumphant and mobbed by an encircling crowd in 3 min 59.4 sec ... ". He goes on to note the "intelligent enthusiasm" of the small crowd during the last lap when it was realised that "something big was about to be recorded by the time-keeper". He appears not to accept that conditions were "unpromising" and opines, "actually, the weather was fine for the race". After referring briefly to the results of two early events in the match, he names the teams for the one-mile and outlines the running of the first three laps of the race. He then writes:

"At the bell, Chataway was still a little in front of Bannister and one had to wait again for the back-stretch to see a new and decisive phase in the race unfold itself. Bannister now lengthened his magnificent stride and, obviously going very fast, passed Chataway and raced farther and farther ahead.

"Spectators now really sensed a triumph of above the average and as Bannister broke the tape some 50 yards ahead of Chataway there was a general swoop on to the centre of the field. Bannister was encircled and disappeared from view, but somehow the news leaked out. There was a scene of the wildest excitement ... ".

The same issue of *The Times* also carried an article on the history of the one-mile record – "Stepping Stones to the Four-Minute Mile". Readers were reminded that "the four-minute mile is a milestone, not a finishing post" and the article ended:

> **"So the matter of the four-minute mile rested up to last evening. Bannister's performance, if formally ratified, will earn for him athletic immortality, no matter how soon someone else goes a fraction of a second better – or even a shade better than that."**

The praise and admiration were there, of course, but the sense of elation seemed somewhat restrained.

The *Daily Telegraph* produced an expert account of the race in a two-column article by Jack Crump, Secretary of the BAAB, which included a much larger picture of Bannister's final stride. Crump wrote:

> **"This great triumph by an English athlete on an English track – Bannister ran on the Iffley Road ground where he learned his running as an undergraduate – took the sporting world by surprise. It came at the start of an athletic season in America and in Europe where several runners ... planned final assaults on the 'even-time' mile."**

He also reported, much in contrast to *The Times* correspondent, that:

> **"Bannister's historic run was all the more remarkable because it was his first public race this season, and the chilly and blustering wind made conditions far from ideal for record breaking."**

His description of the race itself is very well informed. He praises the front-running of Brasher and Chataway, and describes the last lap so:

> **"All round the last lap the crowd roared encouragement to the runners and when Chataway slowed with 250 yards to go, Bannister strode into the lead, quickly opened a gap and, appearing not even to be strained, sprinted to the tape in fine style to win the race in 3 min 59.4 sec."**

Crump spoke with Bannister soon after the race and was assured that the lap times were "almost exactly what he had hoped". The report is garnished with some statistics from Hägg's record run in 1945 and some earlier mile record times. It has an authoritative ring about it in spite of the "appearing not even to be strained" comment, a view no other reporter shared, and still makes very good reading.

The *Guardian Journal* (now no longer published) carried the story under the heading "'Dream' Mile Comes True. Magnificent Run in Poor Conditions". According to this report "conditions were all against a four-minute mile" and Bannister himself is quoted as saying "the conditions are stupid". The last few hundred yards of the race are described so:

> **"He showed, despite obvious signs of the terrific strain under which he was going, that he was making the four-minute mile his goal and cheered on by the crowd, he tore up the final straight to get home a brilliant winner. Immediately he had passed the tape pandemonium broke loose for the crowd jumped from the stands, rushed across the track and the exhausted runner, supported by officials, was soon the centre of a milling and admiring crowd."**

This reporter's impression ("obvious signs of the terrific strain") contrasts oddly with that of Crump (above).

Other 'dailys' (some, alas, now defunct) (including the *Daily Herald*, the *Daily Mirror*, the *News Chronicle*, and the *Daily Sketch*), each in its own idiosyncratic style, gave full coverage to the epic event, with copious illustrations and brimming with praise. Noteworthy quotes from these and other reports are:

> **"From an athletic standpoint this is as historic as breaking the sound barrier."**
> **(*Daily Herald* – a comment form Arthur Daley, *New York Times* sports columnist.)**

> **"Bannister will never do it – his training methods are all wrong."**
> **(*Daily Herald*, quoting views of unidentified 'experts' before the race.)**

> **"I don't believe a lot of races are necessary."**
> **(*Daily Herald*, quoting Bannister after the race.)**

"I think the four-minute mile has been over-rated."
(*Daily Herald*, quoting from Bannister's Sportsview interview after the race.)

"I felt pretty tired at the end."!
(*Daily Mirror*, quoting Bannister.)

"This is great, great, great. Bannister is a great runner."
(*Daily Mirror*, quoting John Landy's reaction to the news.)

"I might have done two seconds better except for the wind."
(*News Chronicle*, quoting Bannister.)

"and a few minutes before the start it was agreed we should have a go because we thought the Americans might be making another attempt this week-end."
(*News Chronicle*, quoting Bannister.)

"The crowd stormed the track to congratulate him. But at that moment his legs gave way under him. Two officials had to hold him up."
(*News Chronicle*, Athletic Correspondent.)

"Nature gave him the right bony frame for the job. Will-power and unceasing effort did the rest...Yet all this training, physique, feeding and experience can only be combined successfully by force of character."
(*News Chronicle*, Medical Correspondent.)

"The excitement of this occasion, for those of us lucky enough to see it, will live in our minds forever."
(Unidentified cutting – by H.J. Oaten.)

"It was a great performance. Of all milers Bannister is the one I would just as soon have seen break four minutes."
(*The Times* (8 May 1954) quoting Wes Santee's reaction to the news.)

"It will rate not only as a new world record but also as the sporting achievement of the century. And it was achieved in unfavourable conditions."
(Unidentified cutting – by Terence O'Connor.)

Joy was unconfined. Perhaps the loudest cheers came from the *Daily Express* (with the *Daily Mail* a very close second). The 'banner' heading "At Last – The 4-min. Mile" spanned the full width of the front page, and reports and pictures took up well over half the page (the *Express* was then in a 'broadsheet' format). The main article ("English victory beats world") sets the scene – "a cold damp evening with lightning streaking far off", initially "a 20 mile-an-hour crosswind" then a lull and "a double rainbow over the (St John's) church". The account continues:

"What was he trying? Experts had said it was impossible ... Santee was trying hard in America and Landy in Australia – and Bannister wanted to put Britain there first. For the past three weeks he had been sitting for examinations."

Then the start, the first three lap times, and

"He didn't know how fast he was running. But he ran the lap in 58.9 sec – and ran straight on into the almanacs of glory.
"He finished against the wind, fighting for breath, his head rolling with fatigue – and, as he broke the tape, he fell headlong.
"He was unconscious – and so the last man at the track to realise his success."

No one else had picked up on the rainbow or the examinations!

In a second article alongside the main one, Bannister ("as told to a *Daily Express* reporter") talks about the final stages of the race and gives some general comments on records and racing, and on what the rest of the season might hold.

There was also a full-width headline across the back page – "Bannister conquers 4-minute mile" – introducing "the story of the race, with a lap by lap commentary" by Desmond Hackett. Readers are taken through the laps again and "the hatchet-faced Bannister's" struggle round the last bend and along the finishing straight. Two more articles fill out the story – "'Brainy' Doctor Pips the World" by Frank Rostron and "Weight, stride and oxygen intake make him No. 1" by Chapman Pincher.

Nowhere in this abundance of front and back page reporting was any reference made to the other runners, Hulatt, Gordon and Dole. The silence on Dole is particularly noteworthy. Only the previous day, writing in the *Daily Express*, Bob Pennington had harped on about the "poker-faced American George Dole", his "consent" to the outcome of the race and his "dilemma" in deciding whether to do what was best for his team or to help Bannister. On the day, these matters, previously crucial, did not warrant a mention!

8. Ratification

When an existing record for an athletics event is bettered the improved time (or weight, or height, or distance) does not automatically become a new record; it has to be ratified. This process entails a scrutiny of all relevant details by the appropriate authority, acting independently, to ensure that the submission is authentic and that all the regulations and requirements have been complied with. Only when this process has been satisfactorily completed can a claim for a new record – an 'official' record – be approved.

For Bannister's mile the sequence was described as:

> **"First it (the time) must go to the AAA records committee, then to the full general committee. This meets today (Saturday 8 May), but unless the records committee meets specially beforehand, the claim will have to wait for a month, until the next full meeting. Then it goes forward to the international body – and will have to wait for their routine meeting ..."**

Writing in the *Daily Telegraph*, Jack Crump refers to Bannister's mile time of 4 min 2 sec which failed to gain ratification in 1953 and adds:

> **"There is no danger, however, that his time this evening will fail to be ratified by the International Amateur Athletic Federation. Three official timekeepers certified the time and the race was run in a properly constituted match between the AAA and Oxford University, and was on a track that measured half an inch more than the required 440 yards.**
> **"At Oxford tonight the world record application form was completed**

by officials of the British Amateur Athletic Board, who will formally submit the performance for ratification without delay."

On Saturday 8 May, two days after the race, *The Times* Special Correspondent wrote:

"There seems little doubt that Bannister's time will be ratified. It was stated on behalf of the British Amateur Athletic Board yesterday that it will be sent forward to the International Federation for recognition and 'not the slightest trouble' is expected."

Ratification at national level was confirmed in *The Times* of Monday, 10 May 1954. The Amateur Athletic Association accepted the time of 3 min 59.4 sec as a new English Native record, and the British Amateur Athletic Board also approved the time as a new British All-Comers and British National record. The AAA and BAAB had clearly acted with great expedition. (In 1953 the BAAB had taken two weeks to disallow the 4 min 2 sec time for the mile at Motspur Park and over two months to ratify the 4 min 3.6 sec time from the OUAC v. AAA match.)

Ratification by the IAAF followed shortly afterwards.

It is interesting at this time to return to the ratification process and to look again at some of the considerations facing those involved. Re-reading Bannister's account of his reaction to the disallowing of his 4 min 2 sec mile at Motspur Park in 1953, it would appear that an indispensable criterion for ratification was that the time must be achieved in a bona fide competition in which all runners set out to finish, i.e. by implication, no runner is included for the purpose of assisting another runner to achieve a fast time. In plain words, the competition must be a genuine race and pace-making is out. There can be no doubt that the race was 'genuine' in that it appeared in the match programme as part of a major athletic competition. The question of pace-making, however, is not so readily resolved. Inadvertently or not, several press accounts include the expression. The *Daily Herald* story has a sub-heading "The Pace-Makers" and the *Daily Sketch* refers to "Pace-maker Chataway". In the *Daily Express* Chataway is quoted as saying "I knew that the plan we had practiced on all winter was taking place ... My job was to take Roger to the three-quarter-mile mark in three minutes and ..." Jack Crump writes in the *Daily Telegraph* that "Brasher nobly assumed (the) role of pace-maker", and it cannot be assumed that he would not understand the risks inherent in the use of the word. In reporting Landy's new record (The Times, 22 June 1954) both Brasher and Chataway are referred to specifically as "pace-makers" in the Iffley Road mile.

The expression persists in non-contemporaneous accounts. In an article by Duncan Mackay entitled 'The History Man' in the May 1994 issue of *Runner's World* one reads:

> **"The plan they had come up with involved Chataway and Brasher setting the pace and shielding Bannister from the elements. Pace-making was officially frowned upon, but ..."**

and

> **"When Brasher completed his duty – he was eventually to jog in towards the back of the field – Chataway kept the momentum going."**

In the same issue Bruce Tulloh, the well known long-distance runner (and a sub-four-minute miler), uses the sub-heading "Roger Bannister had pace-makers when he broke the world record" in an article entitled "Making the Pace".

The entry for Bannister, Sir R.G., in the 1998 Edition of the Cambridge Biographical Encyclopedia reads "... he became the first man to run the mile in under 4 minutes (3 min 59.4 sec), with the help of pace-makers ...".

Notwithstanding these observations and in common with athletics enthusiasts worldwide, we remain very happy that the ratifying scrutineers were clearly able to agree that there had been no infringement of the (then) current rules and that a new record had been established, and history made.

9. Memorabilia

Not a great deal remains by way of memorabilia from this historic event. We know of several autographed programmes and there are almost certainly others, perhaps forgotten. There are some fine large wall pictures in the new Iffley Road stand. John De'Ath assures us that during the 40th anniversary celebrations in 1994 the starter's pistol and the St George's flag which had flown on St John's Church tower had 'appeared', but there seems to be some uncertainty about their present whereabouts. We are told that two of the watches used to time the mile were sold at auction to Lord Archer, the author and ex-deputy chairman of the Conservative Party.

10. Landy and Vancouver

There this account might finish, but two other instalments beg to be added – Landy's new world record in June 1954 and the 'Miracle Mile' at the Empire Games in Vancouver in August 1954.

The outstanding performances of Wes Santee and John Landy and the motivating pressure brought on to Bannister as a result have already been mentioned. After 6 May the question became who would be the second person to break four minutes? Santee produced times short by only a fraction of a second, but the next sub-four-minute miler turned out to be Landy.

Finland, home country of a string of brilliant runners and host country for the 1952 Olympics, boasted excellent track facilities and near-perfect conditions for mile running. Landy had taken himself off there in the spring of 1954, bent on finding that extra edge that would take him inside four minutes. (At that time he had no fewer than six mile times inside 4 min 3 sec to his credit.)

Some weeks after the Iffley Road mile Chris Chataway decided, rather to Bannister's surprise, to go to Finland to race against Landy, and it seems that it was largely due to him that the race was run over a mile rather than 1500m. They ran on the Olympic track in Turku on Monday 21 June in 'nearly perfect' conditions – 'there was a slight head wind in the final stretch and the track was dry'. Landy took the lead in the second lap and, 'driven on' from behind by Chataway, he pulled away eventually to win by some 45 yards in a new world record time of 3 min 58.0 sec, an incredible 1.4 sec inside Bannister's time. He is reported as saying that "it was just a competitive race" and that he had no plans for going for a record, but it was precisely the competition that had gained him that fractional increase in speed for the new record. Chataway finished second in a new personal best time of 4 min 4.4 sec. Bannister had held the world record for just 46 days.

Some further comments on the world one-mile record and the changes in the record through the twentieth century are included in Appendix I.

It is difficult now to recapture the excitement in the air through the early summer of 1954 at the prospect of a race between Landy and Bannister. Here were two young men in their prime, the present and previous holders of the world one-mile record, the only runners in the world to have achieved a sub-four-minute mile, held in the very highest esteem for their sportsmanship and fine personal qualities as well as for their running. What a race if they could run together. The 'clash of the giants' came at the Empire Games in Vancouver – the one-mile final was scheduled for Saturday, 7 August, the two heats having been completed two days before. The story takes up five pages in the penultimate chapter of Bannister's book.

There were eight runners in the line-up. (Chataway did not run in the mile! He contented himself with a gold medal in the three-miles in a new Games record time of 13 min 35.2 sec.) Bannister "was really looking forward to" the race. His thinking was that Landy would try to run him into the ground, and he reckoned that if he could run evenly he might have a greater reserve left at the finish. The setting was perfect. Landy took the lead half-way round the first lap and completed the lap in 58.2 sec with Bannister some seven yards behind in 59.2 sec. Landy built up his lead considerably in the second lap, which Bannister completed in 59.8 sec. At this point he had almost lost contact with Landy and felt compelled to quicken his stride so as to cut down Landy's lead before the on-set of the final lap. At the bell he was at Landy's shoulder, having completed the third lap in 59.6 sec (2.7 sec faster than his Iffley Road time). This was the ideal position for him at this point, but the question remained – had he the reserves of strength to hold Landy and then overtake him in the closing stages. Bannister writes "I fixed myself to Landy like a shadow". He hung on as Landy quickened his stride on entering the back straight and held him through the straight and round the final bend, passing the 1500m mark in a time equal to Landy's world record (3 min 41.8 sec) for the distance.

Bannister recalls "with each stride now I attempted to husband a little strength for the moment at the end of the bend when I had decided to pounce". He found the strength to fling himself past Landy just before the end of the bend. The timing was exquisite. At the same moment Landy glanced over his left shoulder, saw nothing, and lost a vital fraction of a second (and the psychological battle) in responding to Bannister's challenge. "In two strides I was past him" writes Bannister, and he just managed to keep ahead and reach the tape with a lead of 5 yards in 3 min 58.8 sec. (Bannister ends his account with a word for the gallant marathon runner Jim Peters who entered the stadium reeling with exhaustion and was allowed to continue until he collapsed 200 yards short of the finishing line.)

Bannister's lap times of 59.2, 59.8, 59.6 and 60.2 sec showed a remarkable consistency, with a difference of only one second between the fastest and slowest laps. In the Iffley Road mile this difference was 4.8 seconds.

The crowd was delirious, their expectations having been vastly exceeded. There had probably never been a finer mile race. Two men, the best in the world, in competition against each other, and both finishing inside four minutes. The times though hardly mattered. It was a superb race and many would agree that it is this result, rather than that at Iffley Road, which provides a true measure of Bannister's unsurpassed greatness as a mile runner.

Note added after reading the typescript

On our first read through the typescript we noticed, with something approaching embarrassment, that our accounts of Landy's record mile and the Empire Games mile contained no mention of any of the runners other than the first two placings! We'd been swept along with the same kind of concentration we had seen in Bannister's book and in the numerous other reports of the Iffley Road mile. The lesson there for us had not been learned. Who knows of the other runners who gave of their utmost in these races and now never rate the merest mention? The least that might be done here is that we give all the runners and their placings in these two events.

The full results for Landy's record mile, as given in the 1995 compilation *Progression of World Best Performances and Official IAAF World Records* were:

		min	sec
1.	**J.M. Landy**	3	58.0
	(all three watches read 3 min 57.9 sec but this was rounded up to 3 min 58.0 sec under prevailing IAAF rules)		
2.	**Chris Chataway (GBR)**	4	4.4
3.	**Olavi Vuorisalo**	4	7.0
4.	**Denis Johansson**	4	7.6
5.	**Ilmari Taipale**	4	10.6
6.	**Aulis Kallio**		

The final placings in the Empire Games mile, as recorded in Bannister's book were:

		min	sec
1.	R.G. Bannister (England)	3	58.8
2.	J. Landy (Australia)	3	59.6
3.	R. Ferguson (Canada)	4	4.6
4.	V. Milligan (N. Ireland)	4	5.0
5.	M. Halberg (New Zealand)	4	7.2
6.	I. Boyd (England)	4	7.2
7.	W. Baillie (New Zealand)	4	11.0

D.C. Law (England) retired, having lost a shoe.

The 5 sec (35 yards) gap between the second and third runners is noteworthy.

1.   Beginnings
2.   Tibshelf
3.   Ann
4.   Other sources
5.   To Iffley Road

THE SEARCH

"Now, what I want is Facts ...
Facts alone are wanted in life."
Charles Dickens (Hard Times)

1. Beginnings

John De'Ath and Arthur Keily had led us to W.T. Hulatt (Alfreton). We were intrigued and with no sure idea of where our enquiries might lead us we set off to find out more about him. Our 'home base' was Derby and long before discovering W.T.H. we used to meet there from time to time and go for long walks along the Derwent valley and over the surrounding countryside, sampling the pub lunches and generally putting the world to rights. The search began on a dismal drizzling December day. After an unrewarding visit to the Derby Local Studies Library, we drove off to Alfreton, about half an hour's journey, to see what might be available there. We parked the car and struck off through the rain, across the town centre, to the local library.

We asked the lady at the enquiry counter if the library had any information about the Alfreton Athletic Club or about W.T. Hulatt, a member of the club who had been a prominent runner in the 1950s. She found a catalogue and began to thumb through it, successfully concealing any enthusiasm she might have had for the task. A colleague who had overheard our enquiry produced two wallets of press-cuttings on local activities, which she thought might be helpful, and a third lady volunteered the name of a teacher at an Alfreton school who might have known something of the Athletic Club. It was a start. We took the catalogue and the press-cuttings through to the main part of the library and began combing through them. The catalogue was not helpful but before long among the press-cuttings, we came across our first 'find'.

It was a picture of a group of about twenty young members of the Alfreton Athletic Club at a club dinner, which had appeared in a local newspaper (the *Echo*) in July 1994. The photograph seemed to date from the 1950s. It had been provided by a Mrs Margaret Stocks (née White) from nearby Selston, who had joined the club in 1951. The story read:

"Plans to keep alive the memory of Tibshelf runner Tom Hulatt have brought back memories for Margaret Stocks ...

"There were so many good athletes among us. Tom Hulatt was the best and a gentleman."

Margaret is in the group but Tom is not. A Freda Hunt is mentioned in the text.

As we photocopied this cutting in the front part of the library, the third staff lady appeared. We showed her the cutting. Yes, she said, she knew of Tom Hulatt and Tibshelf and Selston, and she knew Freda Hunt. She seemed about as pleased as we were with the find. We were tidying up the cuttings on our table when, much to our surprise and delight, the staff lady came through with the news that Freda Hunt was on the phone, would we like to talk to her! We leapt at the chance. Here was a contact with someone who would almost certainly have known Tom Hulatt. It was a pleasure to talk with her. Yes, she had known Tom. He'd lived in Tibshelf, down the lane opposite the church; she'd been to the house for tea. He had worked on the railway. He didn't marry. He died in the 1990s; obituaries had appeared in the local newspapers, the *Derbyshire Times* and the *Chad*. She mentioned a Percy Norman as a prominent figure in Tom's early years. All this was music to our ears. The conversation had to end, but we left our phone number with Ms Hunt who said that she might contact us again if she was able to remember more.

That was not the end of our good fortune. Our library lady mentioned that the library held issues of the *Chad* newspaper back to 1990 and, though this was not ordinarily allowed, we could look through them. She took us through to a locked room, an inner sanctum, with shelved boxes of *Chads* and other papers, and allowed us to stay there and look through them at our leisure. Each issue comprised six-to-eight pages of local news, including an occasional obituary, followed by twenty-to-thirty pages of classified advertisements and a back page of sports news. After perhaps half an hour of searching we found an obituary for Tom Hulatt in the issue of 1 June 1990; he had died on 21 May

1990. (We reproduce the obituary in Part III.) This 'discovery', sad though it was, was the first firm step in our attempt to build up a picture of W.T. Hulatt (Alfreton). We took a photocopy, returned our *Chads* to the appropriate box and left the room as we had found it.

We thanked the library staff and returned to Derby, very heartened, with two wonderful finds and several possible lines for furthering our search, including a contact for the Alfreton Athletic and Sports Club which the first library lady had found for us. We also knew that Tom had lived in Tibshelf. It had been a very good first day and our appetites were well and truly whetted.

Before following up the leads we had uncovered we agreed that we should extend our trawl by placing a notice in the *Chad* newspaper asking that anyone with knowledge of Tom Hulatt should contact us. This we did; the outcome is dealt with in the next section.

The text with the *Echo's* picture of the Alfreton A.C. club dinner had mentioned "Plans to keep alive the memory of...Tom Hulatt". We have not been able to find out what these plans amounted to in 1994 nor what became of them. We contacted the Alfreton Athletic and Sports Club man whom the library lady had identified but this led nowhere. Later on, Tom's friend Cyril Leason of Pilsley mentioned to us that it had been proposed that some form of commemorative stone or plaque should be positioned on the Five Pits Trail and he indicated to us where this might have been placed – at the point where the trail crosses the Tibshelf-Pilsley road just outside Pilsley. However, permission to install such a memorial required the approval of four planning authorities and little progress had been made.

The *Echo* picture had been provided by Margaret Stocks who lived in Selston, about three miles from Alfreton. We telephoned Margaret and she was very happy that we should visit her to talk about the early days of the Alfreton Athletic Club and what she could remember of Tom Hulatt. She had joined the club as a junior in 1951, with much encouragement and support from her father. There were then only two club members, Freda Hunt and Tom Hulatt; Margaret was the third! She recalled names and events from the early 1950s. She was younger than Tom but she had known him; her brother had known him too and her father often used to talk with him. Margaret and her husband were very hospitable and helpful; it was a pleasure to chat with them. They let us borrow a pile of old match programmes from the early 1950s that Margaret's father had marked up and in many of which Tom Hulatt's name appeared.

Margaret was no longer in touch with Freda Hunt and we had some difficulty in re-establishing contact with her. We spoke with her eventually but she could not add to what she had already told us.

We contacted local newspapers. *The Derbyshire Times* provided a photocopy of a very informative article dated 14 May 1954, based on an interview with Tom Hulatt and entitled "I ran in Bannister's record mile. Alfreton man's eye-witness account of greatest day in athletics." The article also included some information on A.D. Gordon, one of the Oxford team members in the first four-minute mile race and son of Dr J.D. Gordon of Bolsover, Derbyshire. The *Derbyshire Times* had also published an obituary in the issue of Friday, 1 June 1990. Cuttings from the *Derby Evening Telegraph* included a short article (dated 7 May 1954) on Tom Hulatt, together with an account of the deluge of telegrams and phone calls that Bannister and his parents had to cope with; an item on his (Tom's) move to London to join the Polytechnic Harriers later in 1954; and a brief note on his absence from the 40th anniversary celebrations in 1994.

A search through the microfilm records held in the Manchester Central Library produced no obituaries or announcements of Tom Hulatt's death in the national newspapers.

2. Tibshelf

Our notice in the *Chad* newspaper calling for information on Tom Hulatt appeared in the 19 January 2001 issue, all but lost at the bottom of page 11, sandwiched between adverts for Wedding Photography and Clairvoyant Readings. Not surprisingly, the notice produced only one reply! It became clear later that there was no shortage of people in the Tibshelf area who had known Tom Hulatt and we were left wondering about the circulation of the newspaper and, perhaps more significant, the extent to which it was read. As it turned out however, that single reply brought about all we could have wished for at this stage of our search.

The reply came from a Mr Terry Watts. He phoned to say that he had not been close to Tom himself but his mother had known him and one of his sisters might be able to help us. We contacted her and she advised us to get in touch with a Mr Cyril Leason, who lived locally and was possibly the best source of information on Tom Hulatt available. We found a C. Leeson, Tibshelf, in the local phone directory (the Leason/Leeson distinction had escaped us up to this point) and rang the number. We found we had contacted Christine Leeson!

We mentioned why we had phoned. She knew nothing of Tom Hulatt but she assured us that a Mr Cecil Hill, a retired Tibshelf farmer, was an expert in local history and would almost certainly be able to help us.

So, our next phone call was to Mr Cecil Hill. He was most forthcoming. Had he known Tom Hulatt? Yes, Tom was a good runner but he wouldn't practice. He'd started running at the Tibshelf Flower Show after the war. He (Cecil) had a videotape of one of the early shows and Tom might be on it. He had a sister, Ann, who still lived in Tibshelf. (We were elated with this news and recognised that here was the break-through we had been seeking.) Could we come to see him? Yes, of course. He gave us directions to his home, Ashmore Farm. Do you know Tibshelf? No! There's only one street, High Street. Come along past the Crown, past the Royal Oak, then on the right you'll see two stone gateposts and a white five-bar gate to Ashmore Farm. We went there the same afternoon.

This was our first visit to Tibshelf. (Its claim to fame is that it was the site of Britain's first inland oil well.) We took the right turn at the bottom of the hill outside Alfreton on the Chesterfield road and aimed for Tibshelf. We were under an overcast sky; the narrow road was hemmed with bare hawthorn hedges and successive straggles of houses. The directions we had been given were just right and we spotted the gate and the farmhouse without difficulty. We took the liberty of parking in the Royal Oak car park and made our way over to Ashmore Farm. This was a fine old Derbyshire longhouse; it was a cold cheerless winter's day but there were pansies in flower in the front garden.

Cecil Hill welcomed us in and drew us to a blazing fire in a handsome stone fireplace in his front room. He was relieved to hear that we were Derbyshire born and bred as we introduced ourselves and told him about our interests. He certainly knew of Tom Hulatt and his family, and readily shared his recollections with us. Their house, originally built for the railway workers who had constructed the line through Tibshelf, was in Westwoods, approached along Church Lane opposite the church. It seemed that the family had not been particularly well off. Tom had trained along the railway track towards Pilsley. Later he (Cecil) would take us to his friend next door who had known the family very well. At this point Cecil's daughter, Margaret, called us into the kitchen where she had set up the videotape of the 1956 Tibshelf Flower Show. It was a gem. It ran for over half an hour, all to-ing and fro-ing, local dignitaries, men in flat caps, old fashioned cars, torrenting rain, fur and feather, dahlias, duck eggs, Victoria sponges, running and cycle races. Cecil looked hard with us while we watched but he could not pick out Tom Hulatt anywhere. Be that as it may, the video had captured the lost flavour of these events wonderfully.

Before Cecil took us round to his neighbours, Margaret told us that Tom Hulatt had been mentioned in a *Daily Telegraph* sports article written by Donald Trelford in a summer issue between 1993 and 1996. Where this nugget came from we were not to know, but we did manage to find the article(s) (see Part III); they told us little about Tom but they highlighted the fallibility of the press.

Cecil hurried us through the drizzle along the road to the next house to meet his neighbour Colin Croft. Again we were made very welcome. Colin was a very fit 84-year-old who still took care of his 1/3 acre garden. The Crofts had been dispensing chemists in Tibshelf for many years until Colin retired. As a result he was very well known locally and, more to the point, he had known practically everyone in the neighbourhood.

He had known the Hulatts very well and at one time Tom's father, Harry, had worked for Colin's father; he (Harry) had also been in demand as the local rat-catcher. Colin recalled giving his old train set to Tom's father as a present for Tom. Tom had been in the Army. Colin told us about Tom's close friend, Cyril Leason, who had been a great help to Tom's sister Ann in organizing Tom's funeral. He (Cyril) had also tried to organise a memorial plaque for Tom but nothing had materialised.

Colin gave us Cyril's address and phone number so that we could contact him directly. Then, out of the blue, he offered to telephone Tom's sister Ann so that we could speak to her. We could hardly believe our luck. In a trice, after Colin had introduced us, we were talking with her. She could not have been more friendly and without a moment's hesitation she agreed that we could visit her to talk about Tom. We fixed on the Wednesday of the following week. We thanked Colin, walked back to Ashmore Farm with Cecil and then to the car park.

Cecil and Colin had been incredibly helpful and we were thrilled with the progress we had made, all stemming from Terry Watts's response to our *Chad* notice! We were especially pleased to have contacted Ann and looked forward to meeting her with a shared sense of excitement.

We visited Tibshelf (rendered locally as "Tibshuff") and the surrounding area many times after this first visit to talk to Ann and Cyril Leason, and to meet other friends of Tom. Our 'forward base' for these visits was the Blue Bell Inn, Alfreton, and we came to greatly appreciate the shandies (shades of Vincent's Club – see Part I) and bar-lunches served there.

3. Ann

Ann lived alone in a small bungalow in a quiet cul-de-sac at the far end of the village. She made us welcome from the moment she opened the door. "You're Peter" she greeted us "and you're Paul. Come in." There was no question of 'breaking the ice'; she was at ease with us and, as a consequence, we with her from the very beginning. She ushered us into the front room and sat us down as we confirmed who we were and what we were about. She was spry, smiling and alert. When we were settled she stood with her back to the coal fire in the open grate and asked us if we would like a cup of tea "or even a glass of wine". Tea, please. She bustled about to and fro into the kitchen while we chatted about Tom; she'd asked Cyril Leason, Tom's good friend and hers, to come over from Pilsley to join us. This was a very welcome move; it would be much better for us to see them together.

It was wonderful to talk with her. First she cleared up the question of names. She was Ann; really her name was Annie, the same as her mother's, so to avoid confusion she was always Ann. The family name was Hulatt spelt so and pronounced as in 'hew' not as in 'hull', though even some Tibshelf people had it wrong. (Some time later we did hear of "Tommy 'ulatt", and in this form, surprisingly, it comes off the tongue more readily with the wrong pronunciation than with the right.)

She produced a copy of the original Iffley Road match programme autographed on the front by Tom's three team-mates Bannister, Brasher and Chataway – this had been Tom's. Tom's brother Harry, who had been with him at Iffley Road, had given her his programme – this she had given to Cyril Leason. (After our meeting with Ann, Harry's daughter, Annette, told Ann of another autographed copy of the programme – in South Africa! This must have been Harry's second copy.) She also showed us a copy of the well-known press photograph of the start of the four-minute mile and, incredibly, the two number cards (43) that had been pinned to Tom's vest. Later on she showed us the vest itself. Her pride in these items and her pleasure in showing them to us and talking about Tom were touchingly evident.

Cyril came. He was considerably younger than Ann and seemed quiet and reserved by nature. He and Ann were clearly very dear friends. Ann brought in the tea on a tray and a box of biscuits. She then brought in a chair from the back room and sat with us to enjoy what was perhaps for her an all too rare occasion – to talk about her family. Cyril told us about his friendship with Tom – they were both bachelors – and about their running together along the track of the old Tibshelf-Pilsley railway line. He told us about the Hardwick Hall Six Mile Road Race, a high-profile annual event which he had organised for the last twenty years; he gave us Souvenir Programmes and lapel badges. (Unfortunately the 2001 race could not be held because of restrictions arising from the foot and mouth outbreak.) He told us of his attempt to organise a memorial to Tom in the form of a marker stone along their old training route and he was clearly unhappy that he had not been able to make progress with this proposal.

We talked on through the afternoon and the conversation never flagged. Neither Ann nor Cyril could identify anyone on the *Echo* picture of the Alfreton AC club dinner. Ann confirmed that she had not been invited to the 40th anniversary celebrations of the four-minute mile in 1994; she had only heard about the celebrations from a neighbour who had by chance heard a radio announcement. As we talked Ann would pop out to fetch this and that to show us. She brought in two scrapbooks of press-cuttings and a large envelope of press and personal photographs and took us through them, sparkling with enjoyment and pride. She thought the cuttings had been collected and assembled by her mother and not Tom. Cuttings in the first scrapbook were devoted mainly to Tom's running from about 1949 to 1960; the second scrapbook covered the four-minute mile and Landy's new record run in Turku, Finland shortly afterwards. The photographs were of running events from the 1950s too and there were some group photographs; they had clearly all been kept with very great care.

There was an inscribed wooden wall plaque which Tom had won in 1949 while he was in the Army, two cups and two boxes of medals from his many racing wins; there was a big medal in a velvet-lined box presented to him for his victories in Holland in 1954. All these had been lovingly cared for and were in perfect condition. (We both later mused that had medals been awarded for the Iffley Road mile there would have been an absolutely unique bronze medal amongst these awards.) The last item Ann showed us was perhaps the most remarkable – neatly folded in a transparent wrapper the banded AAA vest that Tom had worn at Iffley Road (Figure 3). She passed it to us; the vest was soft and clean as if it were new. We were enthralled.

The light was fading outside and we had to leave. Ann urged us to come again, she had so enjoyed the opportunity to revisit her brother's great days, and to help us. We took Cyril back to Pilsley and on the way he showed us the point where the Five Pits Trail crossed the road where he had hoped to put the memorial stone. He had been a great help. We had found two people who had loved Tom dearly and who had cherished his memory over the years. We felt truly privileged that they had shared their memories with us.

Of course we went to Ann's again; we also went to Cyril's home several times to talk with him and we visited some of Tom's other friends in the Tibshelf area. We tried to walk down to Westwoods where the family had lived but the route beyond Church Lane was closed as a result of the 2001 foot and mouth outbreak. We first went to Cyril's a couple of weeks after seeing Ann. He was quickly in his element talking about his work organising the Hardwick Hall Race year by year and the numerous friends and contacts he had made in the athletics world as a result. His enthusiasm was infectious. He produced a well-thumbed address book and gave us contact details of a number of people whom he thought would be able to help us as we tried to build up our picture of Tom Hulatt. We met Cyril's brother Eric; he had a rare fund of good stories, which he told with great style. He suggested that we might contact Dr Hunt, a retired local GP who had known Tom well. We found Dr Hunt the same afternoon. He had been an athlete himself – a walker – and had played rugby until a serious leg injury had kept him out. Yes, he had known Tom, albeit not before the early 1960s, and had found him "a very pleasant gentleman". Amongst the further contacts he suggested was Colin Croft who had been so helpful to us already. What we particularly remember Dr Hunt for is that his twin daughters were both successful Channel swimmers!

Looking back, we think that it was about this time that we became determined to write up the story of Tom Hulatt that was slowly unfolding before us. Previously this had been no more than a possibility, which we had mentioned to Ann and Cyril, but now we found ourselves so taken with Tom's character and achievements, and so moved by the depth and genuineness of Ann's and Cyril's feelings that what had been just a notion became a commitment. We were not professional writers of books and there was a fair measure of caution in our resolve; nevertheless we found ourselves pursuing our search with a new and invigorating sense of purpose.

So, when we next visited Ann we asked if we could borrow the scrapbooks. We had just touched on this before but she had not liked the idea very much; they were so precious to her and she hardly knew us. We had asked Cyril to mention the possibility to her and just before we saw her again he had phoned to say that she had perhaps changed her mind. We drove over to Alfreton again, daring to hope that Ann might relent. There were flurries of snow in the air but little of it settled. We called round first to pick up Cyril and en route to Ann's he asked if we would like to see Tom's grave. He took us through the churchyard round to the back of the church to a neatly edged grave in the last row at the bottom of the slope. There was a sprig of holly in the vase which Ann had left there – it would have been quite a traipse for her to get down to the grave.

We arrived at Ann's in the early afternoon. She was at the door straightaway, smiling and excited, with a welcoming hug for each of us. We were soon seated as before, and tea and biscuits appeared as if by magic. Ann was so pleased to see us and she wanted no prompting at all to talk about the family, her parents, her brothers, their cousins in Nottingham and the moves from Westwoods to Babbington Street and then to her present home.

South Africa had attracted her older brother, Harry, and Ann herself. Harry had served in the South African Air Force and Ann had lived and worked in Cape Town from 1948 to 1953. She did not say what had drawn them there nor why she had come back to the family in Westwoods, and, perhaps for fear of appearing intrusive, neither of us asked her. She then found work in Nottingham, travelling to and from there daily by train. Harry died in 1986. She is still in touch with Harry's children in South Africa and the cousins living near Nottingham.

While Ann talked she bustled into a corner of the room and produced for us photocopies of the autographed Iffley Road match programme and Tom's vest numbers, which we had seen on our previous visit. What this had entailed we can only guess but her kindness touched us. She found the press photographs of Tom and his contemporaries again and went through them with us, remembering, wondering, speculating and greatly enjoying herself, with Cyril helping where he could. There was a treasure trove of memories in them. As before, the conversation went on from strength to strength, never stumbling, never failing; our tea went cold and the biscuits survived the day.

We eventually broached the question of the scrapbooks again – might we borrow them? "Oh" said Ann. She got the two books and held them lovingly to her. "Yes" she said at last, glancing at Cyril for his approval, "but you mustn't let anyone else have them." We promised, and she found a bag for them and passed them to us. We knew how much they meant to her and we were greatly heartened that she should trust them to us. In the event we took photocopies of the cuttings and took the scrapbooks back to Ann a week later, exactly as she had given them to us. They proved to be an indispensable reference as we started the task of documenting Tom's running career.

The afternoon had passed and we had to leave. Cyril promised to provide phone numbers for a contact with the Northern Counties Athletic Association and one or two of the ex-staff members of the local senior school who might have useful information. We said our goodbyes at the door. Cyril showed us Hardwick Hall on the skyline behind the bungalow (Bolsover Castle was four miles behind that but out of sight) and we drove him home. With such generous help we now had every incentive to embark on our writing. Our thoughts were that Ann and Cyril were relieved and happy that someone should put their hand to this task before the passage of time made its attainment impossible.

We continued to see Ann and Cyril, from time to time. Ann very kindly allowed us to use some of her photographs for this book. Cyril was a mine of information; he was patient too as we pestered him for what he knew on a myriad of diverse points such as how the AAA selection process operated, how Tom travelled to the different match venues (he had a moped!), Percy Norman's involvement etc., and he continued to provide us with names and contact details of numerous local people who had known Tom. We followed these up as best we were able; most were simply able to confirm that they had known Tom and that they thought well of him. One or two were able to add significantly to what we knew and their contributions are outlined in the following section.

4. Other sources

Wherever we went and whomever we spoke to in Tibshelf we encountered the name of Everard Hesketh. He had lived in Tibshelf all his life and had known Tom Hulatt from boyhood; they had been very close friends, particularly as young teenagers. When we first tried to contact Everard we had difficulty. It transpired that he had been involved in a drugs research trial for a particular form of cancer, for which he had volunteered and he was not feeling too well. A fortnight later he was much better and he and his wife kindly welcomed us to their home. Everard's dealings with Tom had been outside and beyond Tom's athletics, and our talk with him gave us a further insight into Tom's character, which our previous concentration on his athletics career had not provided.

They had been at school together. Tom's parents would perhaps go out for a drink on Sunday evenings and then Everard would go down to the house to spend time with Tom. They did not like the dark lane between their houses and all sorts of strategies were devised to ensure that neither of them had to traverse it alone. Just after Tom had left the Army, as young 'men about town', they had spent a week together on holiday in Skegness. They had each taken the princely sum of £12. Their board had been £1 per day each, leaving them with £5 or so spending money for the week. They'd had a terrific holiday! Tom had been best man at Everard's wedding; it was a formal morning dress affair but minutes before they were due at the church they had only been able to find one pair of grey gloves. Nothing daunted and ever resourceful, they had taken one glove each, coming over in all the photographs (Figure 4) as well turned out as one could wish.

Everard knew, of course, that Tom was a highly rated runner (he was not an athlete himself), but he had no knowledge of how he came to be selected for the AAA team at Iffley Road. He recalled that Tom was perhaps a little headstrong by nature and thought that he might have gone further had he been prepared to listen to advice. Latterly Tom had put on a little weight. Everard thought that Tom's grandmother had been the housekeeper at the original Ashmore Farm. We left Everard and his wife touched by their very evident affection for Tom and the good humour in their reminiscences.

Eric Glover had also been mentioned as a Tibshelf man who knew Tom well and he was very happy to talk with us. He showed us the house on Babbington Street where the family had moved to from Westwoods and he mentioned Tom's concern for the dogs and other pets he kept when they eventually moved on from there. He recalled keeping up on his bike as Tom lapped round the sports ground, now largely built over, and sitting by the huge horse-drawn roller as Tom sucked the juice out of oranges. The village had been practically self-contained, with enough boot and shoe repair work to keep three cobblers busy full-time. They had even had the use of a swimming pool at the Miners Welfare. 'Ratting' had been a popular pastime, with Tom and his father much involved, and 'heading and tailing' (betting on tossed pennies) and 'horseshoes' (throwing a horseshoe around a peg or stake in the ground) had also been popular. There had been something of a 'loner' in Tom and Eric could believe that there had been times when he might not have been easy to get on with. For all that, he was 'genuine' and everybody in the village thought well of him.

By now, thanks to the help and generosity of the people we had spoken with, we had been able to build up a reasonably well-informed picture of Tom, through his running career and later on. However, we wanted to look beyond Tibshelf and we turned to several other sources for information.

First we sought out the other runners (i.e. other than Bannister, Brasher and

Chataway) named in the Iffley Road match programme. The Data Protection Act prevented the Oxford Alumni Office and the Development Office, University College, from passing their addresses on to us directly, but they had this information and they offered to forward letters on to them. Our letters were brief; we wrote that we were seeking information on the life and achievements of W.T. Hulatt and asked for their recollections of events before, during and after the race, particularly concerning Tom, and whether they had kept in touch with him after the race. (We also asked Dole, an American, how he came to be at Oxford, why he was in the OUAC team and what happened by way of celebration after the race.) We were delighted to have replies from each one of them.

T.N. Miller telephoned us the day he received our request. He had not known Tom but he was very happy to chat and he referred us to the account of an interview he had given that had appeared in the commemorative issue of the *Runner's World* magazine in May 1994.

Alan Gordon replied from France and George Dole from Maine, USA, where they live. We are grateful for their permission to reproduce their letters here. Alan Gordon wrote so:

Dear Mr Stanley

Thank you for your letter concerning Tom Hulatt. I cannot help you very much as I had little contact with Tom after the race. In the Four-Minute Mile he beat me on the run-in for third place. (I enclose a *Derbyshire Times* article published just after the race). I don't think that his athletics career developed very much after the race, partly for the reasons cited in the article. He subsequently went to South Africa. (I left the UK in 1962 for Geneva.)....

Yours sincerely
Alan Gordon

(The article referred to is included in Part III.) Clearly he had not known Tom at all well, even though their names sometimes appeared together in match programmes and they had been the 'Derbyshire pair' in a triangular match at Fallowfield, Manchester, just before the Iffley Road match, finishing first and second (see Part III.)

It seemed to us a remarkable coincidence that two of the four-minute mile runners, one in each team, should be from Derbyshire, their homes, Tibshelf and Bolsover, only 5-6 miles apart. Curiosity drew us to Bolsover – a quiet little town lying to the east of the M1 motorway. The over-riding impression that remains in the minds of both of us is how extraordinarily obliging everyone was to whom we spoke. Alan Gordon's father had been the local GP so our first call was to the Health Centre. He was remembered there but of course he had long since retired. We strolled to the local library and talked at the counter with a lady assistant. A man checking out his books further along the counter overheard our enquiry and immediately offered to take us over to what had been Dr Gordon's house and surgery. He led us out of the library, across the main road, over the car park to a big house on the far side that was now used as the Social Services offices. This had been Alan Gordon's home and again the lady we spoke to did all she could to help us. She suggested we called into the Council Offices nearby, where again we met the same patent concern to help in anyway possible. Nothing of immediate use was forthcoming but we left Bolsover very taken with the pleasantness of its residents. We had not been there before though we had seen the tower of its castle on the skyline from the motorway many times. We short-listed it for a longer visit when this book is finished.

George Dole's letter from America read:

Dear Mr Stanley

I can be of little help, I'm afraid, in regard to your main interest, since that afternoon was the only time Tom Hulatt's and my paths crossed, and we were never introduced to each other. There was a strong suspicion that Bannister was going to make the effort, and it did not seem like an occasion for casual socialising. I remember him primarily as being very quiet and focused – my primary impression was one of intensity. I had no contact with him or with other participants after the race other than with Alan Gordon. Everyone else apparently went home, but Alan and I were still students.

As for my own part in the race, I was in it because I had won the Oxford-Cambridge mile the previous March. I had trained very hard for that, but May found me in the middle of my 'schools term', the last term before my final examinations, and running was beginning to be displaced by studying. If I remember correctly, I went back to my digs after the race and got back to work.

I am sure that I did finish, incidentally. I recently located the letter I wrote home shortly after the race (May 10th), in which I told my parents I had finished last in about 4:25. At the reunion in 1994, Alan Gordon placed me fifth with such confidence that I was inclined to believe him, but I would trust my four-day memory more than his forty-year one.

The letter also reminds me that the Bannister mile was the first of five races I ran in three days. University College had a meeting with Queens College Cambridge on the Friday, and the OUAC had a meeting with the combined Welsh Universities on the Saturday, in both of which I ran the half and the quarter.

I was at Oxford studying Hebrew in preparation for the ministry. I had graduated from Yale in 1952 with a Greek/Latin major, and went on eventually to receive a doctorate in Assyriology from Harvard, to serve thirteen years in parish ministry and twenty-seven or so in seminary teaching.

It seems, that is, that about all I can do is add a little color to your picture. If this prompts any further questions, please to not hesitate to write.

Sincerely,
George Dole

Not surprisingly, he could tell us nothing about Tom. It might seem odd that opposing teams were not introduced to each other but that was the form; clearly concentration was everything and nothing could be allowed to break it. We can see that there were no celebrations for him after the match. The only way of reconciling his recollection of his placing (last) with Alan Gordon's recollection (fifth) is to suppose that Brasher did not finish. But there is much to say that Brasher did finish, not least Brasher's own assurance (see Part I). So we must conclude that Alan Gordon was correct in spite of a forty-year time-lapse.

In a later letter Gordon wrote that he too could not "recollect any particular celebration and, like George Dole, I went back to my college where I think I was in time for late hall (the evening dinner)!"

Later on we wrote to Bannister, Brasher and Chataway, but unfortunately they were not able to add significantly to what we already knew of Tom.

Inevitably as our search progressed we found ourselves seeking confirmation of various details and background information relating to athletics events from the 1950s and for this purpose we were pointed to the National Centre for Athletics Literature (NCAL). The NCAL is housed in the Main Library of the University of Birmingham at the Egbaston campus, which has its own railway station, with a frequent service to and from the main-line station, Birmingham New Street. Having cleared the security system (the staff must be heartily tired of references to Fort Knox) we were able to spend several hours in the Centre and look through the uniquely valuable material kept there.

We were particularly interested in the results of the Northern Counties Athletic Association (NCAA) Championships through the 1950s, and we had no difficulty in confirming that W.T. Hulatt had indeed won the one-mile title in 1952 and 1953 in times of 4 min 23 sec and 4 min 24.6 sec respectively. This title had evaded him thereafter (it went to A.D. Gordon in 1956 with a time of 4 min 12.8 sec), but in 1958 at the White City Stadium in Manchester he won the 3000m steeplechase title in a time of 9 min 28.6 sec, which was within the AAA qualifying standard. He was unplaced in this event in 1959 but finished second in 9 min 28.2 sec in 1960. Having been dependent until now on press-cuttings etc., we were glad to see the formal record of these performances. There is a vast wealth of information at the NCAL and the staff are knowledgeable and patient. The secret of success there is to have a clear idea of what you are looking for and to avoid any distractions from your objective; we enjoyed our visit there.

We also wanted to look at the records held by the Derbyshire Amateur Athletic Association (DAAA). With the help of a succession of local contacts, we eventually located these in the care of Joe Keily, brother of Arthur Keily, an ex-international runner himself and currently Honorary Secretary of the DAAA; he kindly allowed us to look through them. The records consisted of several 'wallet' folders and a number of ledger books containing handwritten minutes of the meetings of the DAAA committee and various items of correspondence and other material. The first working committee meeting was held in the Police Headquarters, Chesterfield, on 11 October 1952. We found mention of W.T. Hulatt's one-mile successes in the County Championships of 1953 and 1956. All in all, the material comprised an invaluable historical account of the endeavours and deliberations of a group of dedicated volunteers working together to ensure that their county was properly represented at national level. We found ourselves wondering what would eventually happen to these records and to possibly dozens of others like them over the country that might be lingering in attics and lofts. The NCAL is available, of course, and is doing all it can to look after the material that comes its way but its resources are limited and there seems much to do. We would appeal to club and county association secretaries who see problems ahead in archiving their records to do their utmost to persuade local study centres or county archives and libraries to take them under their wings.

Readers will have seen that our search methods were, of necessity, relatively crude. We were, however, greatly helped by two friends, George Livesey of Wilmslow, Cheshire and Bryn Roberts of Llandudno, who carried out internet searches for us on particular topics. George provided extensive information on the layout and dimensions of the standard 440 yards track which had provided some difficulties for us and which led eventually to our contact with the National Playing Fields Association (NPFA). Bryn found an alternative source of approved track dimensions, information on the Labour League of Youth (LOY), the Oxford University Athletic Club (OUAC) and the Iffley Road ground, various track records and much other interesting material.

5. To Iffley Road

As we became more and more immersed in our work on this book, the pull of Iffley Road became irresistible and we finally agreed that we had no choice but to go to Oxford and see the historic track for ourselves. We telephoned Iffley Road (the University Sports Complex) and spoke with Richard Dodsworth, the Facilities Manager. Yes, we were told, visitors are welcome and we can certainly come to look round. The opening hours are 7.00 am to 10.30 pm! We asked about the four-minute mile memorabilia that might be there and Richard described the photographic displays in the Entrance Hall and the stand alongside the track. He agreed that a further talk with John De'Ath might he helpful and promised to send us a map, which we duly received.

We had first spoken with John De'Ath months earlier when he had named all the runners in the four-minute mile for us. His input was one of two, which had triggered our search in the first place and it was he who had referred us to Paul Willcox, Honorary Secretary of the Achilles Club, who in turn had let us have a copy of the match programme. He had also mentioned at that time that he had a copy of the 1955 edition of Bannister's book containing the signature of every world one-mile record holder since Bannister. (These he had obtained at the 40th anniversary celebration dinner at the Grosvenor Hotel, London, in 1994. The signature of Hicham El Guerrouj, who set the existing record in 1999, followed later.) He would let us see the book if we were ever in Oxford. We realised that a visit to Iffley Road would also be a golden opportunity to meet John De'Ath. We were delighted when he agreed to meet us there and show us the track. He gave us directions – Iffley Road, Jackdaw Lane opposite 'The Old Ale House', turn right 200 yards down, through the car park and we would be there.

We drove down from Derby, Paul's wife Susan at the wheel, and used the excellent Park and Ride facilities to arrive in Oxford mid-morning, in good time for our meeting. With just a pause to get our bearings and agree a rendezvous, Susan went off sightseeing and we strode out along the High and off down the legendary Iffley Road. This had to be the Sports Complex, that must be St John's Church, and yes, here was Jackdaw Lane. We knew we were right when we spotted that the first turn to the right, leading to a small group of newish houses, was 'Bannister Close'. We took the later turn up through the car park and into the reception area of the main building. The young lady there was very welcoming when we explained our business and quickly produced coffee and biscuits for us while we waited for John De'Ath; we clearly had him to thank for our warm and friendly reception. John arrived and introductions seemed hardly necessary; we were immediately at ease together as a result of our shared interests and enthusiasm. He was delightful company and a veritable mine of information on all things athletic and, even more so, on all things Iffley Road. (It transpired that until recently he had had a major role in the affairs of the complex, coordinating the activities of the numerous university clubs that used the facilities there.)

We sat together around the coffee table and John produced from his case his copy of Bannister's book, autographed over the opening pages as he had described. This was incredible. (We wondered that he could carry the book around with him without an armed guard!) Paul spotted 'Kip Keino'; how so, he queried, he never had the one-mile record. John explained that he was at the 1994 celebrations and must have thought his signature was expected as the book was passed round. To our delight, John had produced a photocopy of the autographed pages, which he passed on to us. He also showed us the splendid brochure which had been produced for the 40th anniversary celebrations and a wonderful group photograph of the record holders – many of them somewhat changed in shape and appearance.

Difficult as it was, we had to put aside these fascinating items and move on. John took us through the office and out onto the track. This was it! This was the Iffley Road track where history had been made. St John's Church tower was unmistakable and we thought we could recognise some of the rooftops and houses we had seen so often in photographs of the finish of the four-minute mile. We lingered on the edge and walked over onto the running surface, as John recounted something of the recent history of the track and the demands made on the management team. The present surface had been laid in 1989 and already its renewal was under consideration.

We went into the main stand, which had been carefully modified and reorganised so as to accommodate 499 people, thus avoiding the considerable cost of extra insurance for stands accommodating 500 or more, required as a result of new regulations following the 1989 tragedy at the Hillsborough football ground in Sheffield. Inside the entrance to the stand at the foot of the stairs was a wall plaque bearing the names of the Oxford Olympians and there were large murals of Bannister on the staircase walls. In the upper rooms there were more excellent pictures of Bannister, which were new to us, taken from inside the track. As a facility the stand was clearly well used; the books and papers of a 'sports injuries' class, with some anatomical models, had been left temporarily in one of the upper rooms. John's knowledge of the venue was unrivalled.

The exchange continued as we moved out again on to the track. We told John of our interest in Tom Hulatt and what we were hoping to do. He remembered the heroic performance of Simon Mugglestone in 1990 when he established a new track record in the commemorative mile held to mark the opening of the new track. We made our way back to the main building, passing the first dig for a new swimming pool en route, and reassembled round the coffee table in the reception area. John told us of the memorabilia he had been able to find for the 40th anniversary celebrations – the St George's flag and the starter's pistol – and mentioned the auction of two of the stopwatches. We could have cheerfully spent the whole day listening and chatting but eventually we had to take ourselves away. We had had a memorable day and were hugely grateful to John for the time he had spent with us and for sharing his reminiscences.

We returned to the city centre, found Susan, and browsed happily around Oxford for a couple of hours before taking the Park and Ride bus back to the car and setting off on our return journey to Derby. Just to underline what a marvellous day we had had we broke the journey at the halfway point and treated ourselves to afternoon tea at The Belfry (of golfing fame). We agreed that the visit seemed to have 'rounded off' our search – perhaps from John De'Ath to John De'Ath – and we found ourselves able to continue putting together the story of Tom Hulatt with a renewed sense of purpose and a fresh enjoyment.

PART III
W.T. HULATT OF TIBSHELF

1.   Early days
2.   Before the four-minute mile
3.   Oxford, 6 May 1954
4.   After the four-minute mile
5.   1960 onwards
6.   The press 'remembers'

W.T. HULATT OF TIBSHELF

"The spirit of the time shall teach me speed."
W. Shakespeare (King John)

Biographers can often draw on letters, written documentation and publications relating to their subject but in this case there was no such material available to us. Instead we have listened to the recollections of Tom's many friends and especially of his sister Ann; we have looked through programmes of local athletic events from the 1950s; we have consulted the records of the Northern Counties Athletic Association and the Derbyshire Amateur Athletic Association; we have gone back to the press coverage of Tom's running career – both local and national – and, thanks to Ann, we have had access to two scrapbooks of newspaper cuttings compiled by Tom's mother through the 1950s. From these sources we have put together the following account of the career and achievements of a remarkable man.

1. Early days
William Thomas (Tom) Hulatt was born in Tibshelf, Derbyshire, on 7 September 1930, the third and youngest child of Charles Henry (Harry) Hulatt, a miner, and his wife Annie. At that time the family lived in the Westwoods part of Tibshelf approached along Church Lane, opposite the church. Harry died in 1966, and Annie in 1990, just a few weeks before Tom himself died.

In those days Tibshelf was a thriving coal-mining village, typical of dozens of other similar communities scattered across the Nottinghamshire and Derbyshire Coalfield, incidentally one of the most productive in the country.

There was a main street, with side roads off, half a dozen pubs and a small cinema (The Savoy); there were some fine old farmhouses too, dating from the days when farming had been the local mainstay. There were three mixed schools, Infants, Junior and Senior. Notable also was the sports field, a large open area where cricket matches and all manner of local activities took place. The nearest town was Alfreton. Chesterfield lay eight or nine miles to the north and Derby and Nottingham as far away again to the south. To the west was Matlock and beyond that the handsome hills of the Peak District; to the east were the meagre remains of Sherwood Forest. The village and its surroundings were close to D.H. Lawrence country and, perhaps as well as anyone, he has described the temperament and distinctive traits of people thereabouts.

The life-blood was coal mining. Successive generations of boys leaving school followed their fathers 'down the pit' or into the numerous surface supporting roles and the coal-handling services. The other choices were farm work or railway work. For the girls, there was light textile work or office work in Alfreton or Chesterfield. There were two pits (or collieries) in Tibshelf itself, owned by the Babbington Colliery Co. Ltd., and four more within a few miles of Tibshelf – Grassmoor, Williamthorpe, Holmewood and Pilsley – and they were the corner-stone of the local economy. (All these collieries are now closed, and the railway infrastructure, built to transport the coal to the main consumers, has largely disappeared. In their place, instead of 'a legacy of derelict land', the Derbyshire County Council has established 'The Five Pits Trail' which provides a traffic-free route for walkers, cyclists and horse-riders across the rolling countryside. With careful reclamation and development, the Trail has become a haven for wildlife and numerous plant species.)

The mines certainly provided work, but for the majority of men it was gruelling work under grim conditions and the rewards were minimal. A miner in the 1930s would typically earn £3 to £4 for a 45 hr week. In 1947 just after nationalisation this had risen to perhaps £7 to £8; a pint of beer would then cost 9d (4p); a loaf of bread 2½d (1p) and a good suit of clothes £4 to £5. Amenities that are nowadays taken for granted such as washing machines, refrigerators, central heating, fast foods and television, were completely out of the question – no one had them. Inevitably, during the 1940s, the Second World War brought many additional restrictions and pressures on everyone – shortages, rationing, the demands of the war.

So times were hard during Tom's early days, particularly for parents bringing up a family on one wage. On two occasions as we talked to Tom's contemporaries in Tibshelf we were assured that the family was "poor", and in those days 'poor' meant a standard of living that only aged parents or grandparents can recall now. A kitchen 'range' with an open fire, shared bedrooms and often shared beds, baths on the hearth, an outside lavatory, clothes worn through, then patched and repaired until they fell apart. The unchanging priorities for parents were the provision of food, clothes and a home for their children. Miners were fortunate in having an allowance of concessionary coal at a very much reduced price, so there would always be a fire in the grate, but in practically all households food from the under-stocked shops had to be supplemented with garden produce (potatoes, carrots, cabbages, peas, fruit) and 'back-yard' livestock (fowls, nowadays called 'hens', rabbits and occasionally pigs). Children were entitled to free school milk ($1/3$ pint per child) but only a small minority of schools were able to provide school dinners, and even at 1 shilling and 8 pence ($8^{1}/_{2}$p) per week not every family could afford them. The school leaving age was 14 years.

However, life was by no means all 'doom and gloom'. There were many good things about those days. Perhaps most important, children were not in thrall to 'the box' and the home computer; they made up their own amusements and were free to roam and explore the countryside around them. A far greater proportion of their time was spent outdoors and as a result youngsters were generally healthy and resourceful, and satisfied with simple pleasures. Sport had not been over-commercialised and the 'hooligan' element, now so sickening, simply did not exist. Football in the winter and cricket in the summer were the most prominent activities, with a wealth of active support and participation at local level in the form of school teams, club teams, works teams, pit teams and pub teams. For travelling the great majority of people relied on public transport (private cars were a rarity) – buses and trains mainly – and the services in general were efficient, economical and reliable.

Like Tom, we, the authors, were born in 1930 and brought up in a Derbyshire mining community. Consequently it has been easy for us to re-capture, in the foregoing, something of Tom's early environment. Our purpose in doing this has not been to suggest that Tom's young days were deprived and under-privileged, and that he therefore warrants special consideration. No, our intention has been to sketch a background that may be unfamiliar to a great many people and against which we can provide a more faithful picture of our subject.

Returning to the Hulatts, Tom's brother, Harry was nine years older than Tom. He served in the RAF during the Second World War and eventually made a career in the South African Air Force, retiring as a senior warrant officer. He died in 1986. His adopted son Vernon and his daughter Annette still live in South Africa and keep in touch with his sister Ann. Tom would probably have seen very little of Harry after 1939 and the relationship between them could not have been very close. However Tom would have had the terrific play-ground kudos of having an older brother in the RAF and it was Harry who, back on a rare visit to Tibshelf, went with Tom to Iffley Road, cheered him through to the finish in the mile, and saw him safely home on the interminable overnight train journey from Oxford. This was the first time that Harry had seen his brother run.

Tom's sister Ann was six years older than Tom. One can safely guess at the relationship between a six year old girl and a baby brother. There would be a strong and loving bond there throughout Tom's childhood and youth. Ann left England in 1948 to join elder brother Harry in South Africa, travelling in an ex-troop-carrier with bunk beds in a big communal 'cabin'. She lived with Harry and his family in Cape Town in a converted barrack room with shared washing/bathing facilities, and found work in a Woolworths store. She was there for five years. Then in September 1953 she returned to the UK bringing with her Harry's daughter Annette, then nine years old, to let her sample life in the UK. It was primarily to collect Annette that Harry came back to Tibshelf in time to accompany Tom to Oxford. He went back to Cape Town with Annette in May 1954, shortly after the Oxford mile. It would be while Ann was in South Africa that Tom's outstanding talent as a runner began to emerge.

The Hulatt home, down Church Lane, is no longer there; it disappeared when the huge railway cutting nearby was filled in. It was one of two 'cottages' surviving from buildings probably used by the original railway constructors; these were timber-built with a corrugated iron cladding. The family lived there certainly until the late 1950s, but at some time in the early 1960s they moved to another part of Tibshelf where they stayed until 1989. Home ownership was less common in those days than now; much accommodation was rented and it seems very likely that this was the case for the Hulatts, but it is not known who the owners of the property were.

Tom's early life would have been no different from that of dozens of contemporaries in the village. A close friend recalls some of their engrossments: tending newts in a bath-tub, solemnly smoking tea leaves in one of his dad's pipes and making a mouse-trap to catch mice alive (and succeeding!). He attended the three Council schools in Tibshelf in succession, first the Infants, then when he was seven the Juniors and finally at eleven years of age the Senior School. There seemed nothing particular to distinguish him from his classmates. He was rated 'good at games', but competitive opportunities were few and far between and his real capabilities could hardly have been suspected. He left school just before Christmas 1944 aged 14 years 3 months.

Of course, he then had to find work, if only to contribute at long last to his keep; staying at home without a job was not an option. The pits might seem to have been an obvious choice. His father had been a miner, but he had been buried twice in one day and was adamant that his sons should not face the same risks. (He would not be the first miner with this policy but many sons being wilful and alternatives being few, it was said more often than it came about.) Tom did not go down the pit. He worked first in a wood-yard, and then it seems as a platelayer (labourer) on the railway in Heath or Pilsley (nearby villages). (Details here are not clear. An age of 16 or thereabouts seems young for a boy in this kind of work, but he is described as such in several accounts and Cyril Leason, younger than Tom but a very good friend, confirms that Tom was a platelayer at Pilsley where his (Cyril's) father was the ganger (foreman).)

However, Tom could not settle into his work and in March 1948, aged 17½, he enlisted in the Regular Army. (His brother Harry had made a successful career in the services; Tom may have been following his lead.) His sister, Ann, recalls that he went to Catterick Camp, Yorkshire, and (she thinks) joined the 'Hussars'. (This would be a tank regiment and several armoured units were, in fact, based in Catterick.) Again, these details are not altogether clear, but what does seem certain is that while he was in the Army in the later 1940s Tom 'got the bug' for running and came to recognise his potential as a middle-distance runner. (Ann has a wooden wall plaque presented to Tom as the winner of a 1949 REME (Corps of Royal Electrical and Mechanical Engineers) 880yards event.) Then abruptly, his sister relates, he bought himself out of the Army in 1949 or 1950.

This episode in Tom's early career is puzzling in a number of respects. Following the Second World War (1939-1945), through the late 1940s and 1950s, until 1961, National Service was an obligation for young men at the age of 18. Exemption could be claimed on health grounds or as a full-time student, and there were a number of reserved occupations, mining being a particular example. National Service entailed a period of 18 months (or 2 years) in the Army, the Royal Navy or the Royal Air Force, followed by a somewhat longer period in the Territorial Army or the appropriate reserve. Naturally a number of National Servicemen enjoyed the life and 'signed on' for regular service; that made sense. But why, one asks, should Tom, with a 'free' opportunity to sample service life coming along at the age of 18, choose to sign on as a Regular at $17^{1}/_{2}$ years of age? It was possible for a regular soldier to leave the army by 'buying out', but this was not cheap. (No exact figure is available for the cost of 'buying out'. An ex-military friend has suggested that it might have been as low as £50 or possibly a year's pay, but the state of training of the soldier would be a consideration.) In the event Tom did buy himself out after two years or so.

Why should he do this? What did he find so unendurable about service life, where the opportunities for training and competitive running were excellent? And, perhaps more pointedly, where did he find the money? His service pay would have been 28 shillings (£1.40p) per week (and from this there would always be a mysterious deduction under the heading of 'barrack damages'!). His savings could not have amounted to a great deal and the sum he needed would have meant several weeks of his father's earnings. His grandmother may have helped.

Obviously these questions cannot be answered now with any degree of certainty, but there seems to have been in Tom a restlessness, when many of his friends would have been adapting to or settling into routines that would last for a good part of their lives. Was he a loner? Could he not abide being told what to do, first this then that, day in day out? Who knows? Perhaps there was something in common between that restlessness and the energy that fuelled his running. Let us follow him into the 1950s after he left the Army.

2. Before the four-minute mile

So, a civilian once again, Tom returned to Tibshelf to live with his parents at Westwoods along Church Lane. His brother and sister were in South Africa at that time. Tom found work in one of the local pit-yards loading coal (either 'loose' or in one hundredweight (51 kg) bags) for delivery. It is not clear which of the local collieries he worked at though Williamthorpe and Holmewood are mentioned in the newspaper cuttings – he may have had a period at each. What is clear is that Tom was not a 'miner' – this designation is reserved for underground workers. Tom was a surface worker. Nevertheless the work would be physically hard on a young man, demanding very high levels of toughness and stamina. The pay would have been no more than about £8 per week, less than that for an underground man.

Contemporaries recall that in those early days Tom's motivation might not always have been sky-high and his approach to training and his enthusiasm for it not always what they might have been. Nevertheless, having taken to running, he would know that whatever his natural abilities, if he was going to get anywhere, even only at a local level, he would have to train. There is perhaps a touch of myth-making in press reports that his training consisted of the daily run to work and back (Williamthorpe was about five miles away, Holmewood four miles). He may have done this, but he would have known that he had to work on speed as well as stamina and that track work, or something close to it, was a 'must'.

There was open land around the house and he used to train there. Later on he would run along the old Tibshelf-Pilsley railway track and when he became interested in steeple-chasing he built a hurdle and water jump behind the house for practice. There was also a good grass 'circuit' around the local sports field (site of the annual Tibshelf Show) that Tom used. It has to be remembered that over these early years Tom had no coach or trainer, no training programme or planned racing schedule, and advice only from his friends and other runners he would meet in local competitions. This perhaps suited him; his drive and perseverance came simply from the will to win.

The quality of some of the advice Tom received might be judged from the recipe for a witch's brew of an embrocation that he used to use:

amber oil	3oz
olive oil	3oz
wintergreen	1 1/2oz
thyme	1 1/2oz
witch hazel	2oz
(1oz = 28 gm)	

These details are preserved on a note pasted to the inside of the cover of the scrapbook of Tom's press-cuttings. He had a bottle made up from time to time by the Tibshelf chemist, Mr Croft. Later on, Tom came to value an embrocation prepared from the comfrey that grew in abundance in Cyril Leason's garden.

Other training opportunities came about. Tom's affiliation over the 1949-51 period is given in programmes and press reports as Alfreton LOY. (The puzzling acronym is deciphered as 'League of Youth'. This long-forgotten body organised recreational activities, nominally for young Labour Party supporters. It was disbanded in 1955.) Tom and Margaret Stocks (née White) of Selston were amongst the very early members of this club. It had no facilities of its own but Margaret recalls that members had access to a grass track at Alfreton School and to the school gym. Also, as the club grew, members were allowed to use the grass tracks at Bentinck Colliery and Sutton-in-Ashfield.

1949-1950

The earliest details of Tom's competitive running appear in a local press report on the Tibshelf Floral and Horticultural Society Sports held in August 1949. Tom, who could have been in the Army at the time, won the 880 yards (handicap) in 1 min 58.4 sec. He would then be a month short of his nineteenth birthday. This win signalled a complete recovery from an early season set back in the form of a broken ankle in May. (Such details of Tom's races that we have been able to gather from his press-cuttings, the DAAA and NCAA records and from Margaret Stocks's old programmes are listed in Appendix II. Some of the cuttings are undated but, by and large, the year and sequence given can be taken as correct.)

Very few of these shows have survived to present times, but their role in their day as a cornerstone of village life cannot be over-rated. They were truly spectacular. Planning would fill the year. There would be competitions for all manner of things agricultural, horticultural and domestic, with marquees and a beer tent, dog-show, huge displays of flowers, roundabouts for the children, often a band and choral events and throughout the day a programme of cycling and running events on the central grass track. All proceeds to charity. (We recall a feature of our own similar local show was guessing the weight of a huge block of coal, the size of a kitchen table.) These shows drew in people from far and wide, and the sporting events attracted many fine athletes, often of county standard. It is no surprise that Tom cut his teeth here – it would be an ideal proving ground for him. (Cecil Hill has a remarkable filmed record of a Tibshelf Flower Show from the 1950s, which we have mentioned in Part II.)

There are no other cuttings for 1949 and there is none at all for 1950. This is unfortunate but it is highly improbable that Tom did no competitive running over this period. One has to assume that the cuttings were not taken or were mislaid. There is, however, a good deal of information for 1951.

1951

The early season brought a run of good results for Tom (Figure 5). He won one-mile handicap events at the Riddings Cycle and Athletic Sports in 4 min 9.4 sec, at the Mansfield Festival Sports, Forest Town, in 4 min 15 sec and at a further unknown venue in July. He came second in the mile at the Charity Athletic Sports meeting in Ilkeston. In his second event, the 880 yards, he took second place at the Riddings and Ilkeston meetings and first place at Forest Town in 1 min 53.4 sec for a notable 'double'.

He held his form through August, winning both the mile and the 880 yards at Holmewood, Chesterfield, and, one day later, repeating this success with a 'double' at the Tibshelf Show. (He was also entered for the 3 miles and 440 yards at Tibshelf but there is no record of his competing in these events.) Also in August he is listed for both races at a local National Union of Mineworkers (NUM) Gala. We are unable to date exactly his second placing in the 880 yards event at the Open Meeting and Gala Day of the BSA Sports Club at Small Heath, Birmingham. It would probably have been late in the season and it is noteworthy in that this was Tom's first appearance with Alfreton AC (Athletic Club) affiliation.

Tom had to withdraw from further competition just before the end of the season as a result of a badly twisted knee incurred during the 880 yards race at the Uttoxeter Wakes Sports meeting in September.

Almost all his races had been handicap events, so comparisons on a national scale cannot be made, but by any count this was a most impressive record for a young man who was not 21 years old until the September. Nowadays, it might appear that he took on too much by way of competitive running but there can be no doubting his enthusiasm and talent.

In working through these early press-cuttings one cannot fail to be struck by a pronounced change in style when the staid impersonal hand of a typical local reporter is replaced by something very different. For example, in a brief item on the Tibshelf Show events, one reads:

"Under the careful supervision and keen eye of Mr Percy Norman of Alfreton (manager and trainer) the modest 20-year-old Tibshelf boy is breaking all records on Midland tracks ... Hulatt is undoubtedly a racing machine, with perfect style, controlled and effortless, and times his finishes to perfection ... The whole village turned out in force to see their good local boy keep up an amazing winning sequence."

and for the Forest Town meeting:

> "'Tommy' Hulatt...paid another compliment to his trainer and manager (Mr P. Norman of Prospect Street, Alfreton) when he brought off the 'double' at Forest Town...Timing his finishes to a nicety...Hulatt is undoubtedly one of the racing 'finds' of the season."

and for the Uttoxeter Wakes Sports:

> "Mr Percy Norman, the well-known Alfreton trainer, had got the Tibshelf boy in peak form with the race in view, and just when he was coming through the field in dazzling style ..."

Mr Percy Norman has clearly moved into the picture, and in something of a Svengali role. Exactly what he was able to do for Tom is not clear, but there can be little doubt as to who composed these press contributions. It seems that Mr Norman, a railway worker, was something of a figure in local athletics in the 1950s.

1952

The 1952 season opened with an invitation mile race at the Bournville Sports meeting in Birmingham in May; Tom finished fourth in spite of running "under the supervision of his astute manager and trainer, Mr Percy Norman of Alfreton". It was noted however that he had "wintered well" and that he "looked a racing machine". After winning an 880 yards handicap race in Lincoln a major success followed when he won the one-mile event in the Northern Counties Championships at Billingham-on-Tees (Durham) in June. His time was 4 min 23 sec. In the local reports of this run we are reminded that

> "'Tommy' has been extremely well handled by an astute manager and trainer in Mr Percy Norman of Alfreton,"

but, be that as it may, to become Northern Counties One-Mile Champion at the age of 21 after only two full seasons of competitive running was no mean achievement. Another newspaper, possibly a national one, writes of "the success of unknown W.T. Hullatt (sic) (Alfreton A.C.)". He was 'not placed' in the 880 yards race at this meeting.

As a result of this success Tom was nominated by the (then) newly formed Derbyshire Amateur Athletic Association to represent the county at the Amateur Athletic Association (AAA) Championships at the White City Stadium in London on 20 and 21 June. This opportunity to compete at the highest national level would have been a wonderful experience for Tom. He led the field during the early part of the race but had to drop back later; the race was won by J.M. Landy (Australia) in 4 min 18.4 sec (the same J.M.L. who in two years time would become the second man to break the four-minute mile with a new world record in Turku, Finland.) The possibility, voiced before the race, that Tom's performance in London might take him to the 1952 Olympic Games in Helsinki in July, could have been no more than wishful thinking.

After third place in a one-mile event in Chesterfield and second place in the BSA Silver Trophy 880 yards event at Small Heath, Birmingham, Tom recovered his best form again in the Derbyshire One-Mile Championship event at the Belper Wakes Sports meeting on 7 July, winning from the reigning champion (Eddie Hardy) in a time of 4 min 20.6 sec, a record for the track. He was now, at 21 years of age, Northern Counties Champion and Derbyshire County Champion for the mile.

This was about the halfway mark for the season. Tom went on to win the one-mile and 880 yards events at the British Railways Eastern Region Championship in Essex and, as in 1951, to win both events at the Holmewood (Chesterfield) Sports on August Bank Holiday (Monday 4 August). However, he had to settle for third place in the Tibshelf Show 880 yards and did not run in the mile. We read:

"After a hard season's racing, Mr Percy Norman (manager) very wisely decided not to race his protégé in the mile event ..."

Another meeting at Lincoln is also mentioned where Tom took second place in an invitation mile and he beat Eddie Hardy, the Midland Counties Cross Country Champion, for first place in the mile handicap at the Rolls-Royce Harriers sports meeting in Derby. Altogether, for Tom, 1952 was a full but very successful season and he was just beginning to gain recognition at a national level.

It is unfortunate that nothing can be gleaned from the press-cuttings of Tom's preparation for his running by way of diet, training, resting etc., nor of his mental approach and tactical thinking in his races. His face in press photographs certainly shows toughness and a resolve but one cannot see beyond that. Contemporaries have tried to help us – yes, he was something of an independent spirit, perhaps wilful or even headstrong sometimes, but we cannot see further. His sister was away at this time and his friendship with Cyril Leason lay in the future. The likelihood is that he ran 'instinctively' without a great deal of introspection.

Mr Percy Norman of Alfreton continues to figure prominently in many of the local press-cuttings as Tom's manager and trainer. The constant self-aggrandisement in these cuttings is tiresome and does nothing for Tom. (The writing style in places would be more appropriate if Tom were a boxer or even a racing pigeon.) However, Mr Norman seems to have been very active at the administrative level. From the beginning of 1952, Tom's affiliation is given as Alfreton Athletic Club (the 'Airedale Harriers' affiliation for one of the mile events in the Municipal Sports at Chesterfield must be seen as a programme error); the club Secretary was Mr Percy Norman and he appears to have been largely instrumental in founding the club. Tom was appointed 'Field Captain'. The Derbyshire Amateur Athletic Association also was formed in 1952.

Incidentally, in a cutting announcing his selection for the AAA Championships, Tom is described as a platelayer employed by British Railways at Heath.

1953

The Staveley Iron and Chemical Company's new sports ground at Staveley was opened on 16 May by Lord Burghley, President of the AAA and winner of the 400m hurdles event at the Amsterdam Olympics in 1928. The appearance of the sprinter McDonald Bailey (100m finalist at the 1948 Olympics in London) and five other Olympians on the card gives an indication of the quality of the turnout at this meeting. Tom won the inaugural mile in 4 min 27.2 sec, thereby retaining the Derbyshire County Champion title. (It is perhaps odd that such an important race was held so early in the season. The championship is referred to as the One-Mile Derbyshire AS Championship and no mention is made of the county title he gained at Belper in July 1952.) In June he retained the Northern Counties Athletic Association (NCAA) title he had won at Billingham-on-Tees by winning the championship event held at the University Sports Ground in Hull. The cinder track was reputed to be fast, but Tom's winning time of 4 min 24.6 sec was no improvement on his Billingham time of 4 min 23 sec. He also completed in the 880 yards at this meeting, finishing a respectable fourth.

Tom was included in the NCAA team in a match between the NCAA and the Amateur Athletic Union of Eire held on a windy, blustery day on the Queen's Ground, Chesterfield, in conjunction with the annual Chesterfield Municipal Athletic and Cycling Sports. Tom won the mile race in 4 min 18.2 sec, a time better than that of the winner of the open mile race, Douglas Wilson, an ex Olympic runner. This was on a grass track. The time may have been a personal best for Tom at the time. (A press-cutting mentions that a week later he was to compete in an open mile race at Small Heath, Birmingham, but no details of this event or the match are available.)

As in 1952 Tom was selected for the AAA Championships at the White City Stadium in July, a week after the Small Heath match; he was perhaps disappointed with fifth place in the mile .

There are no press-cuttings for the Tibshelf Sports appearances in 1953, but the programme gives Tom as competing in the 3 miles, the mile and the 880 yards; his affiliation is 'unattached'.

The scrapbook press-cuttings include two references for the latter half of the 1953 season. Tom took second place in an 880 yards race at Clipstone and was second again in a one-mile invitation handicap at Wellington AC Sports Ground. His affiliation for the early part of 1953 (including the AAA championships) is given as Alfreton AC but for these last two events it is given as Mansfield and Tibshelf, respectively.

We emphasise that the prime source of information for the foregoing reconstruction has been the scrapbook press-cuttings, some of which were undated and some with no indication of the source. (Margaret Stocks's programme collection has also been helpful.) The cuttings for 1953 cover fewer events than those for 1952 but it does not follow that Tom's appearances in 1953 were reduced. He may have become more choosy, but it could be that cuttings have simply not been kept. Whatever the case, it will be obvious that our reconstruction of Tom's season is entirely dependent on the information available to us from the press-cuttings and elsewhere; it can be no better. This must be borne in mind in commenting on another feature of the 1953 coverage – the complete absence of any reference to Mr Percy Norman! One notes the apparent affiliation changes and wonders – was there some sort of parting of the ways?

Or are we reading too much into this? It remains something of a puzzle. The positive conclusion for 1953 is that Tom retained both his Northern Counties and Derbyshire County Champion titles and that he could look forward to 1954 with justified confidence in his ability as an established high-class runner.

1954

A three-way match very early in the season took Tom to the Fallowfield Track in Manchester as a member of a Derbyshire AAA team competing against a Christie AC team and a Cheshire County team. The date of this match is not known, but we place it before the Iffley Road mile by perhaps a couple of weeks because no mention of participation in that event is made when "Gordon and Hulatt, the Derbyshire pair" are referred to. Tom won the race in 4 min 24.9 sec pulling ahead of Gordon, his team-mate, in the finishing straight. ('Gordon' was A.D. Gordon of the four-minute mile fame. It is coincidental that at Iffley Road Tom also was to overtake him in the finishing straight; there, however, their placings were third and fourth and they were in opposing teams!)

3. Oxford, 6 May 1954

In our earlier account we have looked at the four-minute mile in some detail, but mainly as seen by Roger Bannister and the national press. Here we look at this momentous event again, but now trying to see the day as Tom would have seen it and trying to re-capture some of his reactions and impressions.

There appears to be no surviving record of the formal invitation from the AAA to Tom to compete as a member of the AAA team in the one-mile event at the OUAC versus AAA match at Oxford on 6 May 1954. We therefore do not know how much prior notice he had. Probably taciturn and undemonstrative by nature, we can only guess at the inner excitement and sense of anticipation he experienced as May approached – to be selected to run at this level and in this company would have seemed 'the stuff of dreams'. We know nothing of his training and preparation; he may have seen the Fallowfield run as a try-out. Oxford could well have been in another world, totally unlike Tom's familiar Tibshelf background. His three team-mates were national figures, representing the cream of middle distance runners at the time. Bannister was a 1952 Olympic 1500m finalist and current British Mile Champion (it's just possible that Tom may have met him at the White City AAA Championships in July 1953 when he finished fifth in the one-mile event). Brasher and Chataway had also competed in the Helsinki Olympics, Chataway finishing a heroic fifth in the 5000m after falling on the last bend. There must have been something approaching awe in Tom's mind as he prepared himself for the day.

Figure 1 – The start of the four-minute mile. Reproduced by kind permission of NI Syndication from The Sunday Times of 1 May, 1994

PROGRAMME *PRICE 6d.*

OUAC

O. U. A. C.

v.

AMATEUR ATHLETIC ASSOCIATION

(UNDER A.A.A. LAWS)

at

IFFLEY ROAD ATHLETIC GROUND

THURSDAY, MAY 6th, 1954, at 5.0 p.m.

6.00 p.m. EVENT 9. ONE MILE.

15. G. F. DOLE (Univ.)
16. A. D. GORDON (Magdalen)
58. T. N. MILLER (Univ.)
41. R. G. BANNISTER (Achilles)*
42. C. J. CHATAWAY (Achilles)*
43. W. T. HULATT (Alfreton)
44. C. W. BRASHER (Achilles)*

1st.................. 2nd.................. 3rd.................. Time......................

Figure 2 – Programme cover and inset, the race details

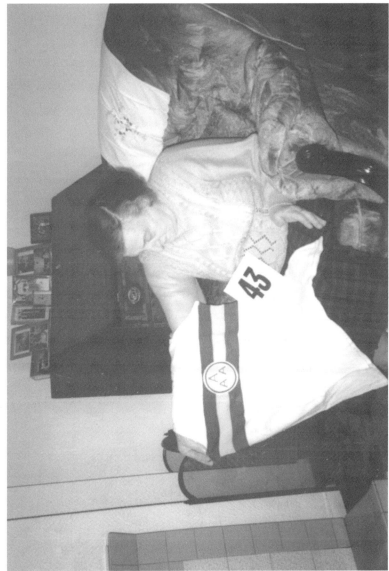

Figure 3 – Ann with Tom's AAA vest

Figure 4 – Sharing the gloves.

Figure 5 – Young Tom

Figure 6 – Leading the field in his AAA vest – probably Tibshelf 1954.

Figure 7 – Gordon Pirie presents the prize for a triple dead-heat (Chiswick 1954).

Figure 8 – Just a sample!

He travelled to Oxford by train, accompanied by his brother Harry. (Tom's mother usually went to meetings with him but on this occasion she stayed at home, perhaps deterred by difficulties foreseen in the very late return journey or perhaps just to give Harry a rare chance to see his talented brother in action.) The Sheffield-London (Marylebone) line passed through Tibshelf and they may have gone via London. Alternatively, they may have travelled via Derby and Birmingham. Whatever their route they would have had no difficulty in getting to Oxford by lunchtime or thereabouts. It is unlikely that they were met at the station; they probably continued on to Iffley Road by bus. The match started at 5 o'clock and the mile was scheduled for 6 o'clock – there may have been a chance to loosen-up on the track in the afternoon.

The nearest we have to a verbatim account of the race from Tom appeared in an article published in the *Derbyshire Times* of Friday, 14 May, 1954, a week after the event. The article is reproduced here in full.

"I RAN IN BANNISTER'S RECORD MILE"
Alfreton Man's Eye-Witness Account of Greatest Day in Athletics

"It was the greatest day of my life," Alfreton miler, Tom Hulatt, told our Sports Reporter on his return from Oxford, where he had been taking part in the historic race in which Roger Bannister became the first man to break the four minute mile barrier.

Hulatt, 23-year-old Tibshelf runner, and A.D. Gordon, 21-year-old son of Dr J.D. Gordon, of Bolsover finished third and fourth in this race, part of the Oxford University v. AAA match on the University track at Iffley Road.

This is how Tom described the event, which has brought Bannister the congratulations of athletes in all corners of the globe.

"There were six of us in the race," said Tom, "four representatives of the AAA and two Oxford men. Fifteen minutes before the event I heard that the attempt on the four-minute mile was off because of the wind, but about ten minutes later the wind dropped a little. Roger came up to me and said: 'Don't hang on to me and Chris (Chataway) – we are going all out. You run your own race.'

"After the first lap, which Roger completed in 57 seconds, I was lying fourth. I knew he was too fast for me. The pace was terrific and I realised that if I was to finish the race I would have to ease off. Roger was running very easy. How he kept it up I don't know. After 2¾ laps Brasher, who had been pacing Roger, dropped back and I passed him. I was lying third with Chataway leading and Roger close on his heels. Gordon drew up and passed me and then I had only one thing in my mind – to beat him. About 300 yards from home I put on an extra bit of speed to regain my former position and came in to finish a comfortable third."

Track in Turmoil
"When I reached the finishing line the track was in a turmoil, with crowds of people swarming to congratulate Roger. He was completely exhausted for a few minutes, and after he had recovered sufficiently I went up to him and shook his hand. Later I got his autograph, and this will be one of my most treasured possessions."

Tom finished about 100 yards behind Bannister. He had, however, recently suffered from a cold and had some slight breathing difficulty — "otherwise I believe I should have been on Chris Chataway's heels," he said.

Typical Reticence
The thing which impressed Tom more than anything about the breaking of the record was the typical English reticence displayed by the spectators. Apart from the first few minutes there was little excitement and the meeting continued as though only a minor track record had been broken. "It was the same at the dinner which followed. There was a strange silence during the meal and practically nobody mentioned Roger's magnificent achievement. Perhaps everybody was too thrilled to talk. If it had been in America the crowds would have been hysterical," said Tom.

Brother Watched
Among the spectators at the meeting was Tom's elder brother, Harry, a member of the South African Air Force, who has been on leave in England for the first time in seven years. Harry, who sailed back to South Africa yesterday on the *Stirling Castle* was seeing his brother run for the first time. "I wouldn't have missed the race for all the tea in China," he told our representative.

Hulatt, who holds the Northern Counties and Derbyshire one-mile championships, is one of the most promising milers in the Midlands. His running achievements are a credit to himself alone, for he has no training facilities except the fields surrounding his home. Employed on coal haulage work at Williamthorpe Colliery, he keeps himself in trim by walking four miles to the colliery at 5.30 every morning and running home at the end of the day.

He believes that the heavy nature of his work – he shovels about 20 tons of coal a day – is preventing him from reaching the top flight of milers. "When I get home my muscles are tight – a big drawback to my training. But my bread and butter must come first, and a light job more suitable to training is hard to find," he added. Until about a year ago Tom was a member of the Alfreton Athletic Club but at the moment he is unattached.

A.D. Gordon

A.D. Gordon is a member of the Chesterfield Harriers and Athletic Club, where his keenness is a by-word.

Gordon, in his first year at Oxford and reading history, holds the Freshman's mile record previously held by Bannister. During his Army service he broke the Egyptian Army mile record. Early this year he was third in the mile against Cambridge at the University Games at White City.

(Reproduced by courtesy of the *Derbyshire Times*)

The account speaks for itself. Even so, a number of details warrant comment. The 'team briefing' from Bannister was indeed brief but Tom appears to have had no other advice on how he might interact with his team-mates, and seems to have had no kind of exchange with Brasher and Chataway. There is a possible hint here that Tom may have known Bannister in that he is the only runner referred to by his Christian name. Gordon, Tom's erstwhile team-mate and fellow Derbyshire-man is mentioned but, not surprisingly, he says nothing of Dole, the second man in the Oxford team. Gordon was ahead of Tom at one point but Tom overtook him to finish "a comfortable third", seemingly a near re-play of the closing stages of the Fallowfield mile. (We guess that 'comfortable' might mean 5 or 10 yards or 1 or 2 seconds.)

Regarding Bannister's autograph, Tom's sister Ann has a virtually pristine copy of the match programme signed on the front by Bannister, Chataway and Brasher. (How a reproduction of this programme could have appeared in a May 1994 issue of the *Derby Evening Telegraph* is a mystery to Tom's sister and his close friends.) Tom could not have got to a copy of the programme until he returned to the changing room and it seems most likely that he persuaded his illustrious team-mates to sign there.

That's not all! It transpired recently that Tom's niece Annette in Cape Town also has a signed copy of the programme and Cyril Leason, Tom's Pilsley friend, has an unsigned original with the times marked in (this had been Harry's, Ann had given it to Cyril). Clearly Tom (and perhaps his brother) must have moved very quickly to get these mementos before the three were inundated by well-wishers and reporters.

Tom refers to "the dinner which followed". It seems unthinkable that the competing teams should not have been fed after their efforts but it would be by no means a 100 per cent turnout. Bannister wrote

"I was to meet the Chrises in London later, and I travelled up by car for a television programme ... We had an evening of celebration."

The programme was *Sportsview* introduced weekly by Peter Dimmock, the BBC Head of Outside Broadcasting. The programme started at 8.20 pm. The exodus from Oxford could not have been much before 7 o'clock so no time was lost in getting to the BBC Lime Grove studios in London. So Bannister and 'the Chrises' would not be at the dinner. In recent correspondence with the authors George Dole writes:

"I had no contact with him (Tom Hulatt) or with other participants after the race other than with Alan Gordon. Everyone else apparently went home, but Alan and I were still students ... If I remember correctly, I went back to my digs after the race and got back to work."

Alan Gordon also confirms that he went back to his college after the match and (he thinks) ate there. It seems possible that Tom was the only mile runner from both teams present at the dinner.

The article notes that Tom is "employed on coal haulage work at Williamthorpe Colliery". A brief account in a local newspaper (the *Derby Evening Telegraph*) published the day after the race describes Tom as "a miner at

Holmewood Colliery"! Inconsistencies of this kind add to the difficulty of reconstructing Tom's working life and career.

It is clear that Tom himself recognised that his heavy daily work moving coal was not an ideal form of training for mile running. He would not have had a wide range of alternatives as a civilian. It has also been mentioned that many club runners would not have planned to reach peak performance as early as May. The Fallowfield event would have been useful but with another couple of months of the season behind him he may have been that much sharper. The cold he mentions might well have taken the edge of his performance. These points are not made as some kind of excuse or to attract a sympathy for Tom; he needed neither. They are mentioned so as to put Tom's performance in a fuller perspective.

It is to be noted that in the match programme Tom's affiliation is given simply as 'Alfreton'. The local newspaper report confirms (after stating otherwise!) that he left the Alfreton AC about a year earlier and was 'now unattached'.

Tom and Harry made their way home from Oxford by train that evening (it has to be supposed that the AAA would not sanction the expenses of an overnight stay in Oxford). The local newspaper account notes that "Mr Hulatt was tired after the all-night journey home". There is no record of a welcoming party at Tibshelf and one wonders how it was that the local newspaper reporter came to be interviewing Tom within hours of his return – perhaps Tom's mother had contacted him.

In none of these contemporaneous accounts is there the slightest hint of any hard feelings on Tom's part. We know that his admiration and respect for Bannister were unstinted and it is hard to imagine that he would have seen his inclusion in such an elite group as anything but a great compliment. Sadly though, according to his friends, there did appear a note of disgruntlement, a sense of having been used.

One friend mentions that Tom felt 'done' when he came back from Oxford because the other runners had started their training two months before; he described the race as a 'set-up job'. Another close friend who knew Tom well surmises that he must have felt 'out of it at Iffley Road' and he could understand why Tom might have felt a little badly about things. It's not difficult to understand these feelings. Obviously Tom would have been thrilled with the invitation and the excitement would doubtless have buoyed him through the run-up to the match and through the day itself. Afterwards, without this sense of euphoria and perhaps in a low moment, the feeling that he was not as well prepared for the race as he could have been might have pressed on him. Perhaps too he was hurt by the virtually complete omission of his name from the flood of the national press coverage of the event on the Friday and ensuing weekend – and in practically all subsequent accounts of it.

4. After the four-minute mile

1954

Immediately after the four-minute mile Tom's affiliation appears as Polytechnic Harriers, the well known London (Chiswick) club. Very shortly after the Oxford race Tom came second in one-mile events in the Rotherham Municipal Sports and in the Bournville Sports, Birmingham; the winner in the Rotherham mile was D. Walker (Sheffield United Harriers). He was not placed in the one-mile at the NCAA Championships in Manchester but, surprisingly, at the Derby and County Athletic Club annual meeting in Derby on 21 June, in "a well judged race against strong opposition" Tom won the open (scratch) three-mile event (from the same D. Walker) by a distance of 40 yards in a time of 14 min 6.2 sec. He did not run in the one-mile event. What had prompted the change of distance is not clear, but all the signs were that Tom had reserves of strength and stamina that the one-mile event did not draw on. The time was only 2.2 sec outside the Northern Counties Championship winning time on a cinder track at Manchester on the previous Saturday. At this time Tom is still referred to as the Derbyshire Mile Champion but it is not known whether he competed or how he fared in the County Championships. Nor do we have any record of him being selected for the AAA Championships in 1954.

A fortnight later Tom finished second, inches behind Ken Wood, in the one-mile (scratch) event at the Belper Wakes meeting after "an extremely fast finishing burst". In mid-July he went on to win the one-mile handicap at the Darlington Combined Sports Association Coronation Trophy Sports; starting off 18 yards, he must have been pleased with his time of 4 min 13 sec. He seems to have lost his form, however, at a small local meeting on August Bank Holiday Monday, organised by the Bentinck Colliery Miners Welfare, when he only managed third place in the mile and was not placed in the 880 yards.

The Tibshelf Show in August again saw Tom in a three-mile event (Figure 6). This was described as "the most thrilling race ever seen at Tibshelf". For the last mile Tom and Eddie Hardy (the eventual winner and winner for the four preceding years) ran neck and neck until, yards from the finish, Hardy made a great burst to finish a yard ahead of Tom.

There followed a very successful trip to Holland as a member of a team from the London Polytechnic Club. Tom competed four times. He won a 1500m event in The Hague in a new Dutch All-Comers' record time of 3 min 57.4 sec (the mile equivalent being 4 min 14.7 sec) and he was one of four Polytechnic men (Dunkley, Evans, Hulatt and Schofield) who finished line abreast as winners of the 3000m team event. Later, in Leiden, he was in the Polytechnic team that established a new Dutch All-Comers' record for the 4x1500m relay, breaking the previous record by 32.2 seconds. The same four runners (Dunkley, Evans, Hulatt and Schofield) then went on to repeat their Hague performance in the 3000m, finishing line abreast again in 8 min 44.4 sec. Tom's equivalent mile time in the relay event was 4 min 11 sec, not far short of his target for the season (see later). To mark his success in the 1500m event in The Hague Tom was presented with a silver medal by the Burgomaster of The Hague. (His sister has the medal. It is a weighty piece some three inches in diameter with the inscription: 11.8.54, 1500m.)

Tom and his Polytechnic team-mates retained their form after their return to England when he, Dunkley and Schofield won an invitation two-mile team event at the Croydon Sports Arena, finishing hand-in-hand in a triple dead-heat in a time of 9 min 9.8 sec. This was a great occasion, sponsored by the *Croydon Times* newspaper and with appearance of leading athletes from Britain, Nigeria and Pakistan. Prizes were presented by Gordon Pirie (Figure 7), the 'Sportsman of the Year', and also present was John Landy of Australia, by then the holder of the World One-Mile Record at 3 min 58.0 sec. Landy was not able to compete but he was presented with a plaque by Jack Crump, the British Amateur Athletic Board team manager, to mark "his perfect sportsmanship off and on the athletic track".

There may have been other end-of-season events after the Croydon meeting. Tom's name appears for the mile and 880 yards events in the programme for the Markham Collieries Ambulance Divisions Sports on 4 September, and a small press-cutting contains a note to the effect that "on 9 October Tom will be running for The Polytechnic in the London-Brighton road race"; there are no details of the outcome of either of these events.

Obviously 1954 was a very significant year for Tom (Figure 8). It might be thought that his selection for the Oxford mile and the confidence in his abilities which that marked would have had the effect of focusing his efforts into a carefully planned schedule of mile racing. But this didn't happen. At Derby in June and again at Tibshelf in August he showed his talent for three-mile running. The new affiliation, Polytechnic Harriers, might appear to be a factor here. If Tom had had the June/July/August period in London he would have had access to a first-class range of facilities and, perhaps more important, to advice and views on his future from some very experienced athletes and coaches. He might have been encouraged to look at new distances and in doing so to have revealed a hitherto unsuspected versatility. (It has to be said that with such encouragement four or five years earlier he might have found his niche elsewhere than in the mile.) But this pattern of events cannot be confirmed. Tom did leave Tibshelf for London but that was not until September. There is no record of where he stayed or how he earned a living. His savings by this time could hardly have been sufficient to live on. The likelihood is that he lived in London, at the most, for a matter of weeks, but there remains an air of mystery over this period.

Tom's own thinking on his move is evident in the following extract from a local newspaper published in August:

> **"In about a fortnight's time Tom Hulatt, 24-year-old Tibshelf athlete, who recently joined the London Polytechnic Harriers, will be leaving his home, 'Westwoods', Church Lane, to live in London.**
> **"Strictly a miler, he hopes that with improved training facilities, he will be able to clip a few seconds off his time.**
> **"At the moment Tom usually clocks between 4 min 14 sec and 4 min 16 sec.**
> **"'I shall be more than satisfied if I can cover the distance in 4 min 10 sec or just under in a year's time' he told the *Telegraph*."**

Apart from the Oxford run, all of Tom's races were in the north or the Midlands until his appearance with the Polytechnic team in Holland in August and his two-mile run in Croydon shortly afterwards. These were very successful outings for him and it is clear that he had integrated well with his new club-mates. It seems, however, that until well into the latter half of the season his Polytechnic affiliation was largely nominal. It did not continue into 1955.

1955

In a one-mile race at Whirlow (Sheffield) Tom (described as the Derbyshire

Champion) came second to Ken Wood, who had produced a record-breaking two-mile performance at the White City the day before! Tom was also second in the 880 yards at this meeting. His affiliation is given as Tibshelf. The Whirlow track was most unusual with a 352 yards lap, i.e. 5 laps to the mile.

Tom was unplaced in the three-mile and one-mile events at the Northern Counties Championships in Manchester on 25 June, but he took the one-mile title at the Welsh AAA Championships on a grass track in Wrexham in a time of 4 min 15.8 sec. This time bettered the previous record for the event but for some unaccountable reason is described as 'unofficial'. Here the affiliation has become Mansfield Harriers. Tom was unsuccessful in a mid-September 880 yards race at the John Player Sports and Gala in Nottingham.

Judging from the press-cuttings alone, Tom's competitive outings in 1955 appear to have been much reduced and the only available one-mile time was short of the 4 min 10 sec he had wanted for the year; his club base seems to have been variable.

1956

There were early successes in 1956 when Tom won both the one-mile and the 880 yards titles at the Derbyshire AAA Championships at Staveley. His mile time was 4 min 17.4 sec, his 880 yards time was 1 min 56.1 sec and his affiliation was given as Tibshelf Athletic Club. In spite of these successes he was unable to get into the one-mile placings at the Northern Counties Championships in late June.

The only other information for 1956 is in the form of a picture taken from the *Sheffield Telegraph* of Monday, 27 August. The occasion is the 'rain delayed' opening of the Sheffield Corporation's new Hillsborough Park Sports Arena on Saturday, 25 August, and the picture shows a group of eight runners splashing through extensive puddles, on a bend of the track. The leader (unidentified) is some yards clear of 'the pack'; Tom, easily recognised in the striped vest he wore at Whirlow and Staveley in the previous year, is lying fourth or fifth. There are no details of the race itself nor of the outcome.

The sparsity of information for this year (and for 1955) is most unfortunate; there is no record of any injuries or illness and it would be unreasonable to suppose that Tom confined his competitive running to only a handful of races.

1957

The story hardly fills out for 1957. In an early inter-club contest, in cold blustery conditions, on a grass track at the Strelley Road Playing Fields, Nottingham, Tom won the 880 yards race in a time of 1 min 58.9 sec. His affiliation had changed again; this time he competed as a Sutton-in-Ashfield club member. This club was second in the two-mile team race and it is possible that Tom was in that event. He appears not to have competed in the senior mile for which the time was 4 min 25.4 sec, a time well inside his capabilities.

Gordon Pirie and Derek Ibbotson figure prominently in a report on the two-mile event at the British Games at the White City, London (and in the evening of the same day in a one-mile race at Watford), but there is no indication that Tom competed in any event at these Games. In late May or early June Tom was third in an exciting invitation mile at Hillsborough Park, Sheffield, won by Mike Beresford in 4 min 11.1 sec, inches ahead of sub-four-minute miler Ken Wood. A surprising item in the detailed results for this meeting reads "3000 metres steeplechase – 1st. Hulatt; – – –; 9 min 26.4 sec". No affiliation is quoted. There is no mention of this in the text of the article and one is left wondering again at the range of Tom's talents – a new event and a win, reminiscent of his three-mile showing at the Derby and County AC meeting in 1954. He had built a practice steeplechase hurdle at his home but whether this was before or after the Hillsborough victory is not known. A contemporaneous account of Tom's thinking at this point would have made fascinating reading. Might it have been that he felt over-shadowed by the number of world-class middle-distance runners around at that time (e.g. Derek Ibbotson, Gordon Pirie, Ken Wood – all sub-four-minute milers) who could give him at least ten seconds? Might he have felt a degree of frustration at his failure to make major meetings or achieve international selection, and decided to look elsewhere? Might new ideas have been triggered by Brasher's steeplechase victory in the Melbourne Olympics? Whatever the case, he had found another event in which he could test himself and, with it, new opportunities.

1958

Tom was now 27 years old, arguably close to or even just past his peak as a middle-distance runner. He might not have rated highly his chances of selection for the Rome Olympics, still two years away, but with the Empire Games in Cardiff in July and the European Games in Stockholm in August it was a big year in athletics and there was much to go for. He opened the season with a great win in the 3000 metres steeplechase in the Northern Counties Championships at White City, Manchester, in June, with a time of 9 min 28.6

sec. His club is listed as Alfreton. Coincidentally at this same meeting Alan Gordon was just beaten into second place in the one-mile race.

This promising beginning was followed by a disappointing third place (off 25 yards) in the one-mile invitation handicap at the Sunderland Police Sports. The winner was the scratch runner Brian Hewson in a time of 4 min 6.6 sec. 'Alfreton AC' reappears as Tom's affiliation at this meeting. Success followed, however, in the 880 yards (scratch) on a rain-sodden grass track at Scunthorpe; the winning time of 2 min 4.6 sec was more an indication of the state of the track than of the runners' abilities. Tom's club is given as 'Chesterfield Harriers'.

Into July, Tom held his form on a rare visit to London when he won the invitation 3000m steeplechase at the Kinnaird Trophy meeting at Chiswick in a greatly improved time of 9 min 9.6 sec, running now as an 'Alfreton and Chesterfield Harrier'. He also regained the Derbyshire one-mile championship at Staveley, near Chesterfield, in a new championship record time of 4 min 15.9 sec, though he was not placed in the 880 yards. These were impressive early season figures and one might wonder at this stage how close Tom came to selection for the Empire Games in Cardiff. There were a number of milers on the scene with times better by 10 sec or more but he had shown great talent in the steeplechase. Unaccountably there was no steeplechase event in the Empire Games! It is possible that this came as a surprise and disappointment to Tom, and took something out of his subsequent performances.

The 1958 AAA Championships were held at the White City Stadium, London on 11-12 July. A thrilling highlight was Brian Hewson's win in the 880 yards over Herb Elliott, 'Australia's wonder miler'. Tom ran in the 3000m steeplechase but could only manage sixth place in a time of 9 min 11.4 sec behind Eric Shirley (1st in 8 min 51.0 sec, a best championship performance) and John Disley (2nd in 8 min 51.2 sec). Top-quality competition and the 'carrot' of European Games selection had not drawn out any improvement in Tom's performance. Practically nothing is known of his training regime or preparation for this important event, and one is left to wonder whether or not he did justice to himself.

About mid-July, Tom won the mile event at an international inter-club contest held in atrocious weather at the Nottingham University Sports Ground. He ran as an Alfreton and Chesterfield Harrier and in conditions of practically continuous rain his time of 4 min 14 sec was commendable.

Teams were now arriving in the UK from the Commonwealth countries for the Empire Games, looking eagerly for warm-up opportunities as they tried to acclimatise to UK conditions before the Games. As a result, a new international element appeared in many otherwise 'ordinary' events. An example was the inclusion of a Nigerian team in a four-team match at Berry Hill, Mansfield. Again, the weather was unkind; it was cold and a major downpour during the afternoon left the arena soaked and numerous puddles and pools on the sodden track. The Universities' Athletic Union team won the overall points title for the match with the Nigerians in second place. The only Nottinghamshire AAA success came from Tom Hulatt who won the mile in 4 min 12.4 sec. (How he came to be running for the Nottinghamshire AAA is not clear.) He also came third in the 880 yards race.

Results are available for an undated (probably August) match between Great Britain and Empire teams, which included a number of invitation events, amongst them the Emsley Carr Mile, won by Murray Halberg of New Zealand, and a 3000m steeplechase in which Tom came second in a time of 9 min 9.2 sec. His affiliation reverts to Alfreton and Chesterfield Harriers.

All the above 1958 events (except almost certainly the last one) appear to precede the Cardiff Empire Games. The press-cuttings for 1958 do not cover these Games nor the European Games in Stockholm. The only later event mentioned in the cuttings is a Synthonia versus AAA match held at the new Billingham Sports Stadium on the afternoon of Saturday 6 September. The highlight of the meeting was the mile which was won by Peter Clarke in the excellent time of 4 min 1.7 sec, then the fastest time for the distance ever run in 'the North', more than two seconds ahead of Graham Everett in second place and Derek Ibbotson in third. Tom, running for Synthonia, took third place in the 3000m steeplechase won by Maurice Herriott in the relatively slow time of 9 min 25.5 sec.

An oddly touching inclusion in the scrapbook are three certificates from the Chesterfield Harriers and Athletic Club awarded to Tom for winning the 880 yards and one-mile events and for gaining the Kelly Cup for "the men's' most meritorious performance in the championship" at the club's annual championships meeting on 14 August 1958.

Looking back through the 1958 season, it might be argued that Tom was not able to maintain his early promise, particularly in the steeplechase event. His victories in the Northern Counties Championships and Kinnaird Trophy match augured well for the season but other wins in the event eluded him. Nevertheless, there is no doubting the very high regard in which he was held; the following closing note to the season appeared in a local newspaper from the pen of an experienced sport correspondent:

"HULATT COULD HAVE FILLED THE GAP"

In spite of having experienced the worst summer within living memory it is comforting to reflect that none of the major sports meetings held in Derbyshire were adversely affected by the weather, and there is every indication that they will all be held again next year, with, I hope, the return of the excellently-organised Church Gresley Miners' Welfare sports, which were sadly missed this season.

On track and road Derbyshire athletes have gained a fair amount of success, and we have every reason to feel proud of such great performers as Peter Wilkinson, Alan Gordon, Jack Metcalf, Michael Bullivant and Arthur Keily, all of whom took part in the Empire Games.

Derbyshire might have contributed yet another international if the English team selectors could have foreseen events in the match with France last weekend.

EXPERIMENT FAILED

Because of a shortage of experienced steeplechasers, Gordon Pirie was selected to partner Dave Shaw, but injured a leg during practice, and Stan Eldon, the AAA six miles champion, was a last minute experimental choice – and he did not meet with success.

Tom Hulatt, of Alfreton AC, who has shown excellent form in steeplechase events this season, could have filled the bill nicely had he been easily available, and I am rather surprised that he has not been selected for the team to meet Finland next weekend in preference to M. Herriott, the Midland Counties junior steeplechase champion.

Hulatt won the Northern Counties title convincingly in June, was placed sixth in the AAA and inter-counties championships, and was second to D. Shaw in the invitation 3000 metres steeplechase at the Great Britain- Empire match last month.

CHANCE FOR HONOURS

I have seen Hulatt in all his big races this year and have been impressed by the ease in which he cleared the obstacles. The cultivation of a little more speed between the hurdles and the ability to go with the leaders could bring him international honours next season.

1959

Tom is now with the Hallamshire club. He was selected as a Derbyshire team member in the 3000m steeplechase at the Inter-County Championships in London at Whitsuntide but nothing is available on his performance. He was unplaced in the Northern Counties 3000m steeplechase at Manchester in June. A faltering start perhaps but success came in the latter half of the year. He won the one-mile race at the Miners' Inter-Divisional Sports at Berry Hill, Mansfield on Bank Holiday Monday and shortly afterwards, running under the 'Hallamshire' flag, he won a three-mile (scratch) event at Roundhay Park, Leeds, in 14 min 16.2 sec. He then produced another one-mile victory, again running for Hallamshire, in an inter-club match at Rawmarsh, Sheffield. This year too he ran in the Chesterfield Harriers and Athletic Club Annual Championships on 20 August, again winning the 880 yards and one-mile events and, incredibly, coming second in the 220 yards sprint. He was awarded the Kelly Cup for the second time for his "most meritorious performance". In a brief report of the prize presentations in Chesterfield, Tom is described as "one of few senior members who, with Derby international distance man Peter Wilkinson, has been coaching the youngsters". This turn to coaching is perhaps to be seen as a new development in Tom's career, suggesting that he recognised that his major successes were behind him but that he had still much to give in this new role.

It is certain that Tom won the 3000m steeplechase at a combined meeting of the Nottinghamshire Athletic Club and the Nottingham Track Association, held at the Harvey Hadden Stadium in Bilborough, Nottingham. In fact, he won the event in two successive years; his times were 9 min 42.4 sec and 10 min 5.0 sec. However we have not been able to determine the years of these events with certainty. There is an indication that they were 1959 and 1960, and the Appendix II entries are given under these years.

1960

Tom now turned his hand to cross-country running and road racing. In early January (probably New Year's Day) he finished eighth in a strong field for the Derbyshire championship over a six-mile course at Kedleston Park, Derby. In April he had found his stride when he won the Hallamshire Harriers club's five-mile road championship for the Hayes Trophy at Rivelin, Sheffield. He also came a close second in 34 min 26 sec in the club's six-and-a-half mile 'sealed handicap' event, being beaten by Tony McGoverne with 'a winning sprint'. He came second in the Northern Counties 3000m steeplechase in a time of 9 min 28.2 sec. The cuttings also record victories as a Hallamshire Harriers club member in two two-mile events, almost certainly in 1960, in times of 9 min 25.2 sec and 9 min 24.0 sec, and in the previously mentioned steeplechase at the Harvey Hadden Stadium in Nottingham. Tom also reappeared at the Tibshelf Sports and came third in the three miles.

Unfortunately, the scrapbook press-cuttings do not continue beyond 1960 (although there is a second book of cuttings largely devoted to Roger Bannister). At this time Tom seems well settled as a Hallamshire Harrier and doubtless still has a good deal of running to do, but we have to rely on other sources, sometimes anecdotal, in following him through the 1960s and beyond.

5. 1960 onwards

Running continued to play a major role in Tom's life. In 1960, together with his sister Ann, he was in a party from Sheffield that went by train to the Olympic Games in Rome. It is unlikely that the visit would have been available in the form of a 'package deal'; someone had had to take on the whole business of planning the route, finding accommodation, handling finances etc. In the event they had no trouble getting tickets and they saw all the heats of the 1500m and Herb Elliott's gold medal run in the final in a new world record time of 3 min 35.6 sec. One is tempted to compare this with what might be involved in getting access to a major international meeting today.

In the early 1950s another local youngster, Cyril Leason, had become interested in running. Cyril was some eight years younger than Tom; his family lived near Tom's home on Church Lane. His father had often seen Tom training over the years and as a result they had established a nodding acquaintance. He mentioned his son's growing interest to Tom and shortly afterwards Tom came round to call for him. From then on an enduring friendship grew between them, with Tom passing on the fruits of his experience and his wealth of knowledge to the young Cyril. They used to train together along a stretch of the old Pilsley – Tibshelf railway track.

It was Cyril who brought Tom to the Chesterfield Harriers club in the late 1950s. Tom willingly took a hand in coaching at the club and very much enjoyed this new involvement with young runners. He continued running himself until a torn Achilles tendon at the age of about 30 put an end to his competitive career. He stayed on in his coaching role, however, with the Chesterfield club. Recalling these times, Margaret Stocks of Selston (an early Alfreton AC member) remembers Tom as always well dressed – typically in a maroon blazer, grey flannel trousers and white shirt – and refers to him as a "gentleman", an accolade rarely conferred in those days, full of meaning, that now seems to have slipped out of use. Tom occasionally accompanied teams of young Derbyshire athletes as a travelling coach/ manager.

The Hulatts (Tom, Ann and their parents) stayed on at their 'Westwoods' home until the early 1960s when they moved to a semi-detached house on Babbington Street, Tibshelf, with a good-sized back garden, ideal for the kennels etc. for the numerous animals and pets which they brought with them. Tom's father died on 2 February 1966.

There is not available a complete detailed record of how Tom earned his living as his running took up less of his time, but it is certain that for some considerable time he was employed by the Derbyshire County Council as a Pest Control Officer, as his father also had been. Much of his work in this capacity involved catching and disposing of the rats that abounded among the farms and derelict pit-yards in the area. Later on, Tom also had his own small business, as a rodent-operative, based in Sheffield and, for a time, at Wilberfoss near York where he had a caravan. He had something of a flare for rat-catching. Cyril Leason's brother Eric recalled an occasion when Tom tilted over Cyril's heavy wooden shed and drew rats bare-handed from the rat-holes under the shed, throwing them to the excited dogs nearby. Tom would then have been in his early twenties. Ratting was a popular local pastime amongst the ex-miners; many had Jack Russells or other terriers for this purpose and would assemble with their mates for the 'sport' when sites were being cleared or buildings demolished.

In the village and surrounding area Tom was always well liked, and many people there remember him as a kindly, modest man. He enjoyed a drink of beer but never more than a pint or so, and he was very fond of the Country Music evenings at his local, the (then) King Edward in Tibshelf (now the NUCS (National Union of Club Stewards) Club). His favourite singer was Slim Whitman.

His friendship with Everard Hesketh survived the years, though contact became intermittent rather than regular. Tom cut a dashing figure as Everard's best man at his wedding in 1964 and he appeared 'out of nowhere' when Everard and his wife were moving into their present home, spending the whole day helping them to move and assemble furniture and to introduce some order into the general chaos usually associated with house-moving. (The plot of land on which the house stands had been bought by Everard's father from St Thomas Hospital, owner of much land in the area. An item in the deeds, dated June 26 1553, reads:

... pitying the miserable estate of the poor fatherless decrepit aged sick and infirm and impotent persons languishing under the various kinds of diseases and also of his special grace thoroughly considering the honest and pious endeavours of ... the Major and Commonalty and Citizens of the City of London ... His Majesty did give and grant unto the Mayor and Commonalty and Citizens of the City of London all that lordship and manor of Tibshelf with all its rights members liberties and appurtenances in the County of Derby.

And ... he ordained that the aforesaid Mayor and Commonality and Citizens should be named and called Governors of the Hospitals of Edward the Sixth King of England and Christ Bridwell and Saint Thomas the Apostle.

Clearly, the lordship and manor of Tibshelf had a long and honourable history.)

Eventually Tom retired from the Pest Control Officer post on ill-health grounds and devoted his time to training greyhounds (with what degree of success we do not know). The family moved from Babbington Street to a bungalow in Tibshelf, in September 1989, and Tom's mother died there in the following April. The move may have left Tom with something of a problem as far as his dogs were concerned. He appears to have spent some of this time in Yorkshire but he was a regular visitor to the bungalow. His sister Ann recalls that he came 'home' from Yorkshire on Friday 18 May 1990 and complained of a chest pain. He was taken to Chesterfield Hospital on the Saturday but discharged himself and came back to the bungalow on the Sunday. He died 'on Sunday evening' and the burial in Tibshelf churchyard took place on Friday 25 May. An obituary from a local paper (the *Chad*, 1 June 1990) is reproduced below.

Miler Tom is Mourned
"Local athletics this week mourned the sudden death of Tom Hulatt of Tibshelf on Monday, 21st May.

Tom, aged 59, was among the top British middle distance runners in his day, winning the Northern Counties Championship Mile three times, as well as the three mile and the 3,000 metres steeplechase.

He was also Derbyshire mile and 880 yards champion, with a best mile time of four minutes and two seconds.

But he will be best remembered for his third place in the first ever sub-four-minute mile race achieved by Roger Bannister in May, 1954.

At the time Tom was a miner at Williamthorpe Colliery, and he would walk the five miles to work, move some 20 tons of coal with a shovel, then run the five miles home.

He was a member of several clubs, including Alfreton AC, Hallamshire Harriers, Chesterfield Harriers and London Polytechnic.

And after Achilles tendon trouble forced his retirement from the track he became coach at Chesterfield Harriers.

Tom is pictured above running for Alfreton and winning a one-mile race from Eddie Hardy of Derby and County AC in 1955.

He never married, but lived with his sister, Ann.

Burial took place at Tibshelf last Friday."

The date in the obituary is given as Monday 21 May. It seems that Ann's recollection of 'Sunday evening' was actually the small hours of Monday morning. We have not been able to confirm the personal best time of 4 min 2 sec mentioned in the obituary.

Our data is not complete but we have no record of a better time for a scratch mile than 4 min 12.4 sec achieved in a match against a visiting Nigerian team at Berry Hill, Mansfield in 1958. Typical times were of the order 4 min 15 sec. Our suspicion is that the value given here should read 4 min 12 sec or that it was recorded for a handicap race.

His death was a consequence of cardiac arrest associated with arterial hardening. Locally, there is sometimes mention of the possible effects of the fumes that may have come from some of the substances used by Tom in his pest-control work but this can only be regarded as uninformed speculation. Cyril Leason shouldered the task of taking care of the funeral arrangements and he placed notices and obituaries in a number of newspapers and magazines. The grave is at the foot of a slope in the churchyard overlooking what used to be the open space, where the Tibshelf Horticultural and Flower Show used to be held.

It is a sad irony that on Saturday 19 May 1990, the day Tom was admitted to Chesterfield Hospital, there was a major celebration at the Iffley Road track in Oxford. The occasion was the annual Oxford v. Cambridge match; a special mile race had been included in the programme to commemorate the opening of the new all-weather track by Sir Roger Bannister himself, then Master of Pembroke College, Oxford. Until 1970 the match had been held at the White City Stadium, London; then, with Iffley Road as the new venue, the one-mile event had been replaced by the 1500 metres. Largely as a result of these factors, Bannister's 1954 time of 3 min 59.4 sec still stood as the track record. (It was also the last of Bannister's many records to remain unbroken.) So, there was the prospect that this venerable record might be bettered. A preview of the event in *The Independent* ("Bannister cannot escape the burden of history"!) reminded readers that sub-four-minute-miles (in 1990) were commonplace, that 585 individuals (including one 17-year-old – Jim Ryun (USA)) could boast such a time, with John Walker (New Zealand) and Steve Scott (USA) each having broken four minutes over one hundred times.

The commemorative mile race was won by Simon Mugglestone, aged 22, of Hertford College, Oxford in a time 3 min 58.9 sec. At long last, a new track record (or at least a new venue record – purists might be disinclined to ignore the change from a cinder track in 1954 to an all-weather synthetic track in 1990). *The Times* of Monday 21 May describes the race:

"When Simon Mugglestone erased the most famous track record from the history books on Saturday ... he still had enough breath to sprint a lap of honour. Just 35 minutes later, he came back to win the university 5000 metres race in 14 min 21 sec."

This was an amazing display of fitness and stamina. Mugglestone said "I feel I've taken a piece of sacred property away." Sir Roger (and John Landy who was also there) had nothing but praise for a wonderful performance. The runner-up was Andrew Geddes in a time of 3 min 59.4 sec, the old track record! Mugglestone and Geddes became the 120th and 121st UK citizens to join the sub-four-minute mile fraternity.

There is a local memorial to Tom and it is in a form that would have given him much pleasure. Year by year since 1981 his friend Cyril Leason has organised the 'Hardwick Hall Six Mile Road Race' over a course from Pilsley School, out to Hardwick Hall and back again to Pilsley. (Hardwick Hall is a fine 'stately home', dating from 1597 and now in the care of the National Trust, some 2-3 miles from Tibshelf. Its building was planned and financed by the indomitable 'Bess of Hardwick' and it is reported to have 'more glass than wall'.) The race has enjoyed the patronage of their Graces the Duke and Duchess of Devonshire and receives generous sponsorship from a number of local organisations. It always attracts a top-quality field from the North Midlands. The Tom Hulatt Trophy is awarded to the first veteran (over 40 years of age) finisher.

6. The press 'remembers'

No national newspapers carried news of Tom's death or any form of obituary, but from time to time both before and after 1990 the press has remembered (or 'discovered') him.

In the early part of May 1979 a 'Profile' appeared in a local newspaper under the heading "When Tom shared the glory". It included the well-known picture of the start of the race (facing p.176 in 'First Four Minutes') together with a picture of Tom, fuller-faced and pensive. The first paragraph reads:

> **"Twenty five years ago on Sunday Tom Hulatt shared in one of the greatest moments in British sporting history,"**

and the article goes on to recount Tom's recollections of "the greatest day of my life". He recalls

> **"It was a cold and miserable afternoon – not ideal running conditions. The weather seemed to be against the attempt until with about 15 minutes to go the wind suddenly dropped.**
>
> **"I remember Roger came up to me before the start and asked me how fit I was. I said that it was really too early in the season for me, so he told me to watch it for the first two laps – in other words to keep out of the way.**
>
> **"I remember staggering over the line in third place, just unable to catch Chataway. By that time there was calamity on the track – it seemed as though the whole crowd was surrounding Bannister."**

Tom remembered Bannister as "a real gent" who "always took time out to have a word with you". (Assuming that the interviewer got it right, one might ponder on the difference between 'gent' and 'gentleman' in this context.)

This is no disgruntlement in Tom's account but it is clear that he thought that he might have been able to do better:

> "I wasn't really warmed up. The AAA championships a couple of months later were the ones we were preparing for. And at the time of the Oxford race I'd got a slight cold."

Tom's hope of AAA selection in 1954 did not materialise, but he must have been pleased to know that his small role in a momentous event was still remembered, if only locally.

It was not until the 30th anniversary of the race in May 1984 that the national press 'discovered' Tom. In a succession of articles on 3, 4 and 5 May the *Daily Express* heralded the 'forgotten man' of athletics. In the first of these pieces, an item entitled "How miner Bill cut a swathe through the three musketeers" was inset into a full-page feature entitled "30 years on ... The *Express* re-runs Bannister's mile". It read:

> "In sporting history, the first four-minute mile is remembered as the race of the three varsity musketeers.
>
> What most people have forgotten about that night at Iffley Road is that there was an interloper among the athletic academics.
>
> He was Bill Hulatt, an almost anonymous miner from Alfreton, Derbyshire.
>
> Running in the vest of the Amateur Athletics Association, Hulatt managed to split the famous names by finishing third in the greatest race of all time.
>
> The almost forgotten W.T. Hulatt came third in 4 minutes 11 seconds and poor Chris Brasher was engulfed by the ecstatic crowd before he crossed the line. His time was never officially recorded."

In spite of the name William, Tom was never called Bill and his time was given incorrectly, but these are just details. Clearly the decision must have then been taken that there was further mileage in this new 'angle'.

The following day there appeared an article devoted to Tom, with the heading "The fastest rat catcher on earth". Tom, "now a spritely 53" and described as the "forgotten man" and "forgotten hero", had been found and interviewed. We are told that:

"Tom's big night came at Oxford on May 6, 1954, when, an unknown miner, he came close to wresting glory from the three Varsity Musketeers – Roger Bannister, Christopher Chataway and Christopher Brasher."

The wrong time appears again and Tom is reported as saying:

"No one remembers that I finished just 50 yards behind Bannister."

(This would have placed him second, ahead of Chataway! The actual distance was about 120 yards. It is not credible that a runner of Tom's experience and integrity could have been so wrong: 50 yards means well into the straight; 120 yards means only just past the middle of the final bend.) The words to Tom from Bannister just before the race are given as:

"Roger came up to me and politely said, 'If you are not fit, just leave it for the first two laps,' meaning keep out of their way, so they had a chance of making every miler's dream ccme true."

The article ends with the information that Tom won 80 of his 200 races and, again, that his fastest time for the mile was 4 min 2 sec.

Whatever one thinks of this kind of article one has to suppose that it 'sells newspapers'. (What it does for Tom Hulatt and for athletics seems not to be a consideration.) Clearly the *Daily Express* thought so because the next day virtually the same article, now with a big picture of Tom with a tugging greyhound, appeared. We read:

"Yesterday the *Daily Express* tracked down the missing star,"

but the missing star has been downgraded in the headline from "The fastest rat catcher on earth" to "The fastest rat catcher in the West".

The 'forgotten man' story reappears three years later in the *Sunday Express* of 12 June 1988, and now, if the gist of the report and the quoted comments are to be believed, a note of vexation does seem to have crept in. The headline is "Forgotten man of the miracle mile" and some of the material appeared in the earlier articles. The new element in the article is a reference to a BBC film that includes a re-enactment of the epic race and in which Tom's role appears not to have been fairly treated. (There is no mention of how the then unfinished film came to Tom's attention.) The scene is set so:

"But hardly had Tom crossed the finishing line than the world forgot him. The record went to Bannister, the accolades to runner-up Chris Chataway and pace-maker Chris Brasher,"

and comments such as "Yet again I've been forgotten" and "... it seems my most memorable moment will end up as a bit part" are attributed to Tom.

These quotes typify the general tone of the article. The authors are well aware of the risk of discounting material which does not support their views, but having formed a picture of the man, they cannot recognise the typical Tom in a number of the remarks attributed to him and they cannot but wonder to what extent they were put into his mouth.

The *Daily Express* returned to the theme in an article of 15 September 1988 entitled "A man who helped make history. The athlete TV forgot in its four-minute mile", apparently after the screening of the film. There is nothing new in the article. The previous mistakes recur: "50 yards behind Roger Bannister"; 4 min 11 sec as Tom's time and 4 min 2 sec as his personal best. Tom is quoted as saying:

"I just kept in the background.
"I'm just proud I was able to take part in the real race, though I wish I'd been fitter."

This seems to have been the last article on Tom Hulatt from that source.

1994 saw the 40th anniversary of the first sub-four-minute mile. The *Derby Evening Telegraph* published a special commemorative article on 5 May entitled "4 minutes of history", a column of which was devoted to "The forgotten man of Iffley Road", Tom Hulatt. It reads:

"But no one ever talks about the runner who finished third. He was William Thomas Hulatt, an unassuming coal haulage worker from Tibshelf, near Alfreton.
"Tom died almost four years ago at the age of 59. He was a born runner and given the lack of coaching facilities and sponsorship of today, he could be regarded as one of the best naturals the North of England has produced."

The reporter had interviewed Tom's sister Ann. She remembered Tom telling them about the tense atmosphere in the dressing room as an attempt on the record was discussed. She mentioned that the race was really too early in the season for Tom. The account continues

"Hulatt ... quietly left the track as Bannister was mobbed by the crowd.
"Tom became something of a local celebrity and our mum and dad were very proud. Ironically the four-minute mile race was on dad's birthday."

The article includes a reminiscence from Arthur Keily, the well-known Derby and County AC marathon runner, in which he proudly recalls out-sprinting 'Tommy' to win a 3$^1/_2$-mile road race. Also, almost as a token of authenticity, there appears a small reproduction of the front page of Tom's Iffley Road programme autographed by Bannister, Chataway and Brasher.

In May 1994 the magazine *Runner's World* appeared as an anniversary issue. In a series of otherwise very good articles Hulatt is mentioned only once (as 'William Hulatt'!). (George Dole and Alan Gordon the Oxford runners also get one mention – in the reminiscences of the non-runner Nigel Miller.)

A Commemoration Dinner was held in London to celebrate the 40th anniversary of the first four-minute mile. A note in the *Derby Evening Telegraph* of 23 December 1993 reads

"A British Athletics Federation tribute to Roger Bannister's historic breaking of the four-minute mile barrier will be missing an important figure.
"For former Alfreton athlete Tom Hulatt, who came third in the famous race, died aged 59 three years ago.
"The Federation had wanted to invite him to a dinner, but Tom's sister Annie .... may attend."

There is a clear indication that Tom's sister, Ann, had been invited to the dinner but she has no recollection of receiving such an invitation. What happened was that Mr Smith, the local baker, told her that he had heard some kind of announcement on the 'wireless' to the effect that the organisers were wanting Tom to join them and were seeking information on his whereabouts. But, of course, by then it was too late.

Everard Hesketh remembers hearing what was probably the same announcement. He telephoned the radio station to be told that someone had rung before him. There seems to have been no follow-up from the organisers to the news of Tom's death.

Tom was remembered, mistakenly as it happened, in the summer of 1995, in "On Thursday", a usually very well-informed sports column by Donald Trelford, which appeared regularly in the *Daily Telegraph*. (His strong points were rugby and cricket, but he had much of interest to say in other fields.) In his piece of 22 June 1995, Trelford noted that Christopher Chataway had been knighted in the Queen's Birthday Honours and suggested that it might now be Brasher's turn. (Roger Bannister had been knighted in 1975 following his period as Chairman of The Sports Council.) "The three ageing knights" might then give us "a glorious lap of honour". Following this suggestion a reader had sent a copy of the Iffley Road programme to Trelford who wrote in a subsequent article:

"There were seven entrants for the mile at 6pm, two of whom, T.N. Miller and W.T. Hulatt, failed to make their appointment with history."

Predictably, a number of correspondents quickly put this right. On 3 August, Trelford wrote:

"Alas, poor Hulatt, the forgotten man of British Athletics ...
"Hulatt not only ran in the historic four-minute mile, but finished third behind Roger Bannister and Christopher Chataway, the other members of the team (sic). The Oxford runners were G.F. Dole, now an American priest, and Alan Gordon ...
"Christopher Brasher, who paced the others, was not selected for the event but persuaded the organisers to include him for the record bid. Some readers say he never finished the race, but he insists that he did ...
"I am not the only person to have been unfair to Hulatt's memory. He was evidently very upset not to be invited to the 30-year celebrations in 1984. The organisers made up for this by inviting him to the 40-year reunion. Unfortunately, he had died, aged 59, four years before. Alas, poor Hulatt, indeed."

So the record was corrected and Tom's role confirmed.

As recently as May 2001, a local monthly publication *Bygone Derby* (an edition of the *Derby Evening Telegraph*) featured a full-page article "The modest miner and the mile of the century" by Sue Williams. Tom is rediscovered once again, and probably not for the last time. However, we have now told all we can about him and our story has come to an end. The telling of it has been a great enjoyment for us and our hope is that this book will serve to establish for Tom Hulatt, as he most surely deserves, a secure and lasting role in both local and national archives as a fine athlete and a worthy competitor.

WORLD RECORD TIMES FOR ONE MILE:
COMMENTS AND OBSERVATIONS

The mile – the statute mile – is the longest unit distance in the imperial measurement system and is now the only imperial (i.e. non-metric) track distance recognised by the International Association of Athletics Federations (IAAF). It is far older than the kilometre, originating supposedly in the Roman unit of one thousand (double) paces (mille passuum.) The mile race has always enjoyed a special standing and esteem in the regard of the public. It is a unit length – plain and unadorned – not an arbitrary sub-division or multiple. The race is over in a few minutes yet it demands and produces the very best in terms of track-craft and tactics. It seems that every stride counts, and no spectator can fail to identify with the runners and share, to some extent, their joys and disappointments at the end. Simply as a record, there is no more to the one-mile record than there is to the long-jump record or the hammer-throwing record, but few would deny the special 'magic' of the one-mile record; it surely represents the pinnacle of athletic achievement.

1. Through the 20th century

The first world one-mile record recognised by the IAAF was the 4 min 14.4 sec run by John Paul Jones (USA) in Cambridge, Massachusetts, in May 1913. (A time of 4 min 12¾ sec had been recorded as early as 1886 by the legendary Walter George, but he was running as a professional and the time could not therefore be accepted as a record.) The succession of improvements on that first record up to the time of writing (autumn, 2001) is shown overleaf:

Time	Runner	Venue	Date
4:14.4	John Paul Jones (USA)	Cambridge, Mass.	31.05.1913
4:12.6	Norman Taber (USA)	Cambridge, Mass.	16.07.1915
4:10.4	Paavo Nurmi (Fin)	Stockholm	23.08.1923
4:09.2	Jules Ladoumégue (Fra)	Paris	04.10.1931
4:07.6	John Lovelock (NZL)	Princeton	15.07.1933
4:06.8	Glenn Cunningham (USA)	Princeton	16.06.1934
4:06.4	Sidney Wooderson (GBR)	Motspur Park	28.08.1937
4:06.2	Gundar Hägg (Swe)*	Gothenburg	01.07.1942
4:04.6	Gundar Hägg (Swe)	Stockholm	04.09.1942
4:02.6	Arne Andersson (Swe)	Gothenburg	01.07.1943
4:01.6	Arne Andersson (Swe)	Malmö	18.07.1944
4:01.4	Gundar Hägg (Swe)	Malmö	17.07.1945
3:59.4	Roger Bannister (GBR)	Oxford	06.05.1954
3:58.0	John Landy (Aus)	Turku	21.06.1954
3:57.2	Derek Ibbotson (GBR)	London	19.07.1957
3:54.5	Herbert Elliott (Aus)	Dublin	06.08.1958
3:54.4	Peter Snell (NZL)	Wanganui	27.01.1962
3:54.1	Peter Snell (NZL)	Auckland	17.11.1964
3:53.6	Michel Jazy (Fra)	Rennes	09.06.1965
3:51.3	James Ryun (USA)	Berkeley	17.07.1966
3:51.1	James Ryun (USA)	Bakersfield	23.06.1967
3:51.0	Filbert Bayi (Tan)	Kingston	17.05.1975
3:49.4	John Walker (NZL)	Gothenburg	12.08.1975
3:49.0	Sebastian Coe (GBR)	Oslo	17.07.1979
3:48.8	Steve Ovett (GBR)	Oslo	01.07.1980
3:48.53	Sebastian Coe (GBR)	Zurich	19.08.1981
3:48.40	Steve Ovett (GBR)	Koblenz	26.08.1981
3:47.33	Sebastian Coe (GBR)	Brussels	28.08.1981
3:46.32	Steve Cram (GBR)	Oslo	27.07.1985
3:44.39	Noureddine Morceli (Alg)	Rieti	05.09.1993
3:43.13	Hicham El Guerrouj (Mor)	Rome	07.07.1999

*Arne Andersson equalled Gundar Hägg's time of 4 min 6.2 sec on 10.07.42. This has not been included above.

It can be seen that over the 86 years between Jones (1913) and El Guerrouj (1999) there were 31 World Record times (i.e. 30 improvements in Jones's time of 4 min 14.4 sec). Twenty three different individuals have held the record, six of them holding it twice or more: Hägg (3 times), Andersson (2), Snell (2), Ryun (2), Coe (3) and Ovett (2). Four runners (Hägg, Andersson, Snell and Ryun) have bettered their own previous record before it had been beaten by anyone else.

The overall improvement in the record time over this period was 31.3 sec; so the average improvement between each new record was just over 1 sec. The greatest improvements were by Herb Elliott (2.7 sec in 1958) and Jim Ryun (2.3 sec in 1966); the smallest improvements were 0.1 sec by Peter Snell in 1962 and Filbert Bayi in 1975, and 0.13 sec by Steve Ovett in 1981.

The average tenure of the record has been just less than three years (2 yrs 10 mths). The briefest tenure was in 1981 when Coe regained the record from Ovett after two days, Ovett having then held it for just one week from Coe! The longest tenures were:

Taber	**1915-23**	**8 yrs 1 mth**
Nurmi	**1923-31**	**8 yrs 1 mth**
Hägg	**1945-54**	**8 yrs 10 mth**
Ryun	**1967-74**	**7 yrs 11 mth**
Cram	**1985-93**	**8 yrs 1 mth**

It is useful to plot the one-mile record times given above against the date of achievement to produce the graph shown in Figure A1, in which the foregoing points of detail are clearly evident. A remarkable feature of the data plot is the more or less constant rate with which the record has been reduced over almost 90 years. One might have expected that over this period it would have become progressively more and more difficult to improve the record time and that the rate of improvement would have decreased, i.e. the data would have followed a flattening curve. This might well have happened had conditions remained constant but, of course, this has not been the case. Important changes include vastly improved running track surfaces and footwear; entirely new training regimes; new understandings of the psychological and physiological elements in sport and of the importance of nutrition and properly balanced diet; a far better medical back-up to cope with injuries; the emergence of sponsorship and greatly enhanced financial rewards; and a widening talent pool as the latent strength of the African countries has emerged. The combined effect of these factors has played a major role in maintaining the steady improvement in world record times, each of which, in its day, was the best ever.

2. The future

Inevitably now questions arise. What does the future hold? How long can the steady improving trend in Figure A1 continue? What will be the world one-mile record in 2010 or 2050 or 2100? Of course, there are no simple answers to such questions; future developments in facilities and training strategies cannot be foreseen, nor can the effects of increasingly attractive sponsorship deals and other incentives. One point, however, is practically certain – the talent pool will continue to expand and probably at an unprecedented rate. In the Introduction to the 1981 edition of his book (which is included in the 1994 edition) Bannister wrote:

> **"With nearly a thousand million Chinese and more than six hundred million Indians waiting in the wings and about to enter the world sports stage, I foresee a continuous and steady progress in athletic record breaking."**

and in the Introduction to the 1994 edition:

> **"The propaganda value of athletic success is immense now that China wants to rejoin the world scene after years of Cultural Revolution and self-imposed isolation..."**

It seems that the Indian sub-continent has yet to find and fully exploit its potential in the field of international athletics, but the award of the 2008 Olympic Games to Beijing is bound to result in a massive new commitment to athletics in China, whose strength, at present, remains virtually untapped. This development will provide a new challenge to countries with an already established standing in athletics, and the overall outcome could be a crop of new records in many track and field events over the early years of the 21st century.

The difficulties in predicting future trends are well illustrated by remarks made by (or attributed to) Bannister himself and others since the 1950s.

A press-cutting from June 1954 entitled "Nearing Absolute Limit" notes that:

> **"Roger Bannister ... once expressed the view that 3 min 58 sec 'was a possibility'. That was ... before his own record effort. After his Oxford run, he revised his opinion ... and thought perhaps a further second could be lopped off."**

The same article reports that Landy's new record time of 3 min 58 sec

> **"is regarded in some medical quarters as the absolute limit to which human endurance can be pushed."**

Just after Bannister's own record run the *Daily Mirror* (7 May 1954) reported that:

> **"Bannister considers that it should be possible to do the mile under proper conditions in 3 min 55 sec!"**

and the *News Chronicle* (7 May 1954):

> **"I (Bannister) am convinced now that a mile can be run in 3 min 55 sec, perhaps even faster."**

Years before, Sidney Wooderson had envisaged an eventual mile record time of 3 min 50 sec, and the day after he announced his retirement from international competition, Bannister is reported as saying that:

> **"there was no medical or physiological reason why men should not run the mile in 3 min 50 sec."**

Events were to prove that human endurance as indicated by these estimates, was nowhere near its limit. The 3 min 55 sec figure was passed by Herb Elliott in 1958, just four years after Bannister's and Landy's records, and 3 min 50 sec in 1975 by John Walker, with no signs of an approaching limit. Bolder thinking was necessary. In the Introduction to the 1981 edition of his book, following his comments on the eventual appearance of the Chinese and Indians on 'the world sports stage', Bannister writes that:

"A 3 min 30 sec mile by the turn of the century is not impossible, provided some harmony prevails in our uneasy world and the sheer stupidity of political chicanery is held at bay."

Whether or not this proviso was met through the 1980s and 1990s is a matter of debate but, with the century well and truly turned, 3 min 30 sec remains a distant objective. In a *Daily Express* article of 3 May 1984, Sebastian Coe is quoted as saying:

"I believe Bannister's record remains one of the greatest performances of all time.
"He would be as much as two seconds a lap faster under today's conditions. Apart from a soggy cinder track he also had to wear heavy leather-soled running shows with spikes sharpened by granite,"

and the reporter adds:

"Coe believes the record will be lowered to around 3 min 40 sec in his lifetime. Bannister is even more ambitious 'I see no reason why we shouldn't break 3 min 30 sec'."

In a separate article in the same issue Coe adds:

"I believe I can run 3 min 45 sec before my career ends."

(He was not far out. His best world record time was 3 min 47.33 sec achieved in Brussels in the summer of 1981. It was to be another twelve years before Noureddine Morceli ran inside 3 min 45 sec.)

Bannister's prediction of 3 min 30 sec appeared again in *The Times* article of 21 May 1990 on Simon Mugglestone's new Iffley Road track record.

In the Introduction to the 1994 edition of his book, Bannister revises his thinking on the attainment of this time. Noting that the record has fallen on average by about 0.3 sec per year, he surmises that:

"At this rate, the 3 min 30 sec mile might be run in the year 2044 – 50 years (from now)."

One can look again at this prediction in the light of the data plot in Figure A1. The 'best-fit' straight line through the full data set from 1913 to 1999 (i.e. the line which best represents the overall trend shown by the data) is included in the figure. The downward gradient of this line is 0.39 sec per year, somewhat greater than the rate of reduction (0.3 sec per year) mentioned by Bannister, and if this rate of change held constant then the 3 min 30 sec time would come about in the year 2028. We can repeat this process using only the data from the second half of the century. Also shown in Figure A1 is the 'best-fit' line through the data from 1954 to 1999. The downward gradient of this line is 0.33 sec per year, less than that (0.39) obtained from the full data set but still slightly greater than the 0.3 used by Bannister. If this value held constant then the year 2036 would see the 3 min 30 sec mile. In both cases, the greater downward gradient results in an earlier prediction.

Results over the last 15 years or so (see Figure A1) appear to suggest that the rate of reduction might be decreasing – possibly to about 0.25 sec per year – but it would be unwise to over-rate the significance of this indication at the present time.

As always, predictions obtained in this way must be treated with caution and none of the above figures is to be taken as exact. The derivation of these years is based on the assumption that the rate of change observed over the past will continue into the future. In this particular case the justification would be that the rate of change has held reasonably steady on average for the best part of a century and there is no compelling reason to suppose that it will change drastically over the next few decades. It remains an assumption, however, and the certainty of the prediction can be no better than the validity of the assumption. Accepting the need for caution we may conclude that it is very unlikely that present-day retirees will see the 3 min 30 sec mark broken, but when today's youngsters are middle-aged or perhaps even grandparents they may have cause to celebrate the attainment of a new landmark in track athletics.

Dare we look forward beyond 2050? For fun perhaps, but not with any serious intention. If the present reduction rate of 0.33 sec per year continues to hold into that period then in about another century we would be looking at a 3 min mile! This can be seen as eighteen successive 100 yds, each run at fractionally over 10 sec and most would agree that it is inconceivable. So there is a limit somewhere but who is to say what it is and when it will be attained. It is a fact that no record in any event – running, throwing, jumping, swimming – has ever proved unbreakable. A record may stand for twenty years or more (e.g. Bob Beamon's long jump of 8.90m (29 ft 2½in) at the 1968 Olympics in Mexico City) but eventually it is always, always broken. We simply do not know and probably never can know what figure – time or distance – in any event represent the limits of human endeavour. And who would want to know anyway?

Looking ahead, it may become acceptable in the future, as one-mile races become rarer, to convert 1500m times to equivalent mile times. This simply requires multiplication of the 1500m time by 1.0729; for example, a 3 min 30 sec 1500m gives an equivalent mile time of 3 min 45.3 sec, an increase of 15.3 seconds.

3. The 'barrier'

It is convenient to refer to Figure A1 in commenting on a detail of usage which is harmless enough but which is irritating to some people – the well established reference to 4 minutes in this context as a 'barrier'. In terms of Figure A1 a 'barrier' would be seen as an unusually prolonged dwell before a new record. Since 1913 there have been five tenures of about 8 years (Taber, Nurmi, Hägg, Ryun and Cram – see above) and the longest of these by a few months was indeed Hägg's tenure of eight years 10 months before Bannister's new record in 1954. But it cannot be overlooked that this period covered the immediate aftermath of the Second World War (1939-45) when many countries were recovering from the massive drain of the war effort and young men had little time or opportunity to concentrate on a well prepared schedule of training and competition. (Sweden, the home country of Hägg and Andersson, was neutral during the war. In 1945 both of these runners were banned from competition for transgressing the amateur rules.) It is not unreasonable that the best part of a decade should have passed before the best international standards reappeared in sport. There may have been a psychological 'aura' about 4 minutes but there is no evidence that breaking that time was unusually difficult. In real terms it was no more special that any other record time. Several athletes were 'in the running' for it at the time (notably Australia's John Landy and Wes Santee of the United States) and the competitive pressure may well have been a help rather than a hindrance. The fact is of course that each and every new record in whatever sport becomes a barrier – it may be surmounted within days or maybe years but in its day it represents a barrier to be broken. To reserve 'barrier' for the 4 minute time is a little unreal. Even Bannister thought that it had been "over-rated". Nevertheless, there is an undeniable 'something' about it and no one would take issue with Peter Wilson writing in the *Daily Mirror* of 7 May 1954:

> **"However many people in the future get inside the magnificent time of four minutes it will always be Bannister's imperishable claim to fame that he was the first to beat the 'time barrier' of 240 sec for 1760 yds."**

4. An alternative presentation

An alternative presentation of the changes in the world one-mile record times is given in Figure A2, which shows the finishing straight and final bend of a 440 yds track. (The old track lay-out has been used with the start and finishing line 20 yds before the end of the straight; the straight has been taken as 90 yds long and, for the purposes of calculation, the bend radius has been taken as 124ft 1⅝ in (see below and subsequently).) In constructing Figure A2, it has been supposed that all the record holders start together in a one-mile race and that each runs at the speed of his own record run with his talents and abilities unchanged in time and without the benefit of any improvements which may have become available since his run. The figure shows the position of each runner on the track at the moment when El Guerrouj finishes.

Taking Derek Ibbotson as an example:

His own record time		= 3 min 57.2 sec
His average speed	= $\dfrac{1760}{237.2}$	= 7.420 yds per sec

Distance run in El Guerrouj's record time:		
of 3 min 43.13 sec	= 7.420 x 223.13	= 1655.6 yds
Distance from finishing		
line	= 1760 – 1655.6	= 104.4 yds

70 yds of this distance will be along the finishing straight and the remaining 34.4yds will be around the final bend. The equivalent angular position (in degrees) around the bend, taken from the junction of the bend and the straight, is obtained by simple proportion as $34.4 \times 180/\pi r$, where r is the bend radius (in yards). For Ibbotson this becomes 47.6 degrees.

Figure A2 is based on a fiction, of course, but it provides an interesting overall picture of developments through the 20th century. One sees, for example, that Jones, the first record holder, would have been almost half a lap (216 yds) behind El Guerrouj. Nurmi, the 'Flying Finn' with 29 world records to his name, would have only just entered the final bend. Bannister would have been about 10 yds behind Landy and almost 120 yds behind El Guerrouj. Herb Elliott, the 'Running Machine' of the late 1950s and early 1960s, would not have been into the straight and Ovett, at his best, would still have had more than 40 yds to go. One can but speculate on how these track positions will shunt backwards over the 21st century!

We emphasise here that our purpose in presenting the record performances in this way has not been to demean past records in relation to the current one or to imply that one record is to be admired more than another – each record in its day represents the pinnacle of excellence – but to provide some kind of overview of a remarkable succession of peak performances.

Regarding our placing of the start/finishing line 20 yds from the beginning of the first bend, there is a curious contradiction on this point in the early versions of Bannister's book which contain a series of excellent photographs. One picture shows Bannister just abreast of Landy in the Vancouver mile at that crucial moment when Landy looks back over his left shoulder; the picture caption is "Eighty yards to go". On pp.215-16 of the book Bannister writes:

"Just before the end of the last bend I flung myself past Landy. As I did so I saw him glance inwards over his opposite shoulder ...
In two strides I was past him, with seventy yards to go."

The final straight was 90 yds long. So how far was the finishing line from the end of the straight, 10 yds (90 minus 80 yds) or 20 yds (90 minus 70 yds)? We opted for the latter, but we could be wrong.

5. Speeds and track dimensions

We digress here slightly to touch upon a number of points relating to mile running in general and the Iffley Road mile in particular. The average speed of a four-minute mile runner is 15 miles per hour (mph); he will cover $7\frac{1}{3}$ yds every second or, put another way, the length of a cricket pitch from wicket to wicket in three seconds. El Guerrouj averaged over 16 mph in his record run. A top-class sprinter moves at more than 20 mph. It is of passing interest to note that a world record miler moves faster than the Oxford/Cambridge crew with the (then current) best time for the annual boat race over four miles 374 yards from Putney to Mortlake on the River Thames. Bannister's average speed in 1954 was 15.04 mph; the speed of the fastest boat race crew up to that time was 14.80 mph (course covered in 17 min 5 sec in 1948). In 1999 El Guerrouj ran at 16.13 mph; the speed of the fastest crew then was 15.49 mph (course covered in 16 min 19 sec in 1998).

The Iffley Road mile in 1954 was run well before the advent of electronic timing. The timekeepers then had to use manually operated stopwatches to record the time lapse between the firing of the starter's pistol and the instant when Bannister broke the tape; they were very experienced individuals, formally approved for the task, and it is noteworthy that each of the three recorded the same time of 3 min 59.4 sec. The stopwatches themselves, of course, would have had to meet specified quality requirements and it is readily accepted that they would have been accurate to 0.1 sec at least. It is not surprising that the ratifying authorities found no problem in accepting the submitted time of 3 min 59.4 sec.

It would also have been necessary to confirm that the track dimensions conformed to requirements, i.e. that the distance run was 1760 yards, and we found ourselves wondering what were the standard dimensions of a 440 yards track in 1954? This information proved surprisingly difficult to get hold of, but eventually our good friends, George Livesey and Bryn Roberts came to our aid; their internet searches produced the information that the standard length of the straights was 270 feet (90 yards) and the radius of the semi-circular bends, measured to the 'track side of the inner kerb', was 123 feet $1^{5/8}$ inches. (Eighths of an inch! We thought these had gone out with quill pens.) In the material which George and Bryn provided, a note was included to the effect that in calculating the track length, an extra foot had to be added to the kerb radius to allow for runners being outside the kerb. With this allowance the calculated track length becomes 439.99 yards. The 0.01 yard deficiency in the track length amounted to less than $1^{1/2}$ inches in a mile.

This information dated from the 1960s and, as confirmation that we needed to go back further, we noted a requirement that for all races from 880 yards upwards, the start should be made from a curved line originating from the inner edge of the track at the end of the straight. (The finish for all races was a straight line across the track at the end of the straight.) This requirement was clearly not in operation in 1954. The well known picture of the start of the four-minute mile (Figure 3) shows that the start was from a straight line across the track which (see above) was 10 or 20 yards from the end of the straight. We clearly needed to look for earlier regulations.

We noted also that the track specification had originated from the workings of a Joint Committee of the National Playing Fields Association (NPFA) and the AAA in 1960. We approached the NPFA. The Technical Director, Jean Wenger, was very helpful and referred us to the 1950 publication *The Planning, Construction and Maintenance of Playing Fields* by Percy White Smith (previously mentioned in Part I). This book gives six alternative sets of dimensions for the 440 yards track, with lengths of the straight varying from 225 ft to 360 ft and with those dimensions given above marked as "considered by athletic authorities as giving the ideal track circuit". It is also confirmed in the book that "the length of any track circuit is measured on a line 1 foot within the track from the inner edge".

All of these details are confirmed in a document entitled *Cinder Running Tracks*, found at the National Centre for Athletics Literature, Birmingham (Catalogue No. NCAL II N26) and published by the NPFA-AAA Joint Committee in March 1954.

There is clearly an arbitrary element in the 1 ft allowance between the path of the runner and the inner edge of the track, but this figure seems entirely reasonable for this purpose. An equivalent allowance of 300 mm is specified for metric tracks.

'On paper' therefore we had now established the nominal dimensions of the Iffley Road track – 270 ft straights and bend radii of 123 ft 1⁵/₈ in. It remained to ascertain the degree of accuracy which might be expected in the actual dimensions, with the track itself, of course, long since gone. A point to have in mind is that a 1 inch error in the bend radii translates to a 0.1 sec difference in timing for a one-mile race. This has been talked through with a chartered civil engineer, well versed in the theory and practice of surveying and site lay-out, David Procter. He is confident that, using the surveying equipment and marking out techniques available in the 1950s, the lap length (including the 1 ft allowance) should have differed by no more than one inch from the nominal 440 yards.

We are assured that nowadays tracks are surveyed periodically to ensure that the dimensions conform with specification. It can be taken that some such form of certification was available for the Iffley Road track when Bannister's time was submitted for ratification.

Three interesting statements on the track length appeared in press reports following the four-minute mile. In the *Daily Telegraph* of 7 May 1954 Jack Crump, then Secretary of the British Amateur Athletic Board, wrote that the Iffley Raod track

"... measured half an inch more than the required 440 yards."

The source of the information is not given. Another unattributed report states, rather opaquely, that:

"The track was surveyed just before the meeting and was found to be half an inch over the four laps."

The *Daily Herald* reporter confides:

"The distance has been checked – and found, in fact, to be two inches over the mile."

The time equivalent of an extra two inches in the distance run is less than one hundredth of a second – unrecordable in 1954 and insignificant.

6. Miscellany

During our preparatory work for this book we came across numerous detailed facts and figures relating to mile running, many of them of interest only to statisticians and archivists. Three points we mention here, however, as being possibly of more general interest.

A mile inside four minutes! Is it thinkable that two miles might be run inside eight minutes or three miles inside twelve minutes? For just how long can a pace of 15 mph be maintained? Some answers are forthcoming. Two miles is not a popular distance and it seldom appears in match programmes; when it does it is usually as a special invitation event. On 19 July 1997 a young Kenyan runner, Daniel Komen, ran two miles at the Hechtel Stadium, Belgium, in a remarkable new world record time of 7 min 58.61 sec. At the time he was 21 yrs two months old. He produced a second sub-eight-minute two mile time (7 min 58.91 sec) at Sydney in February 1998. To date the sub-twelve-minute three mile has not been attained, but that is not to say that it is unattainable. For racing purposes the distance has been almost entirely replaced by the d in following improvements in the three mile time it will be necessary to look at equivalent times derived from 5000m results. The authors remember seeing Ron Clarke run the first sub-thirteen-minute three miles (12 min 52.4 sec) in the AAA Championships at the White City, London, in 1965. The present equivalent world record time (derived from the current 5000m record of 12 min 39.36 sec) is 12 min 13.25 sec. Who is to say what lies ahead?

It has been mentioned that Jim Ryun was the youngest sub-four-minute miler at the age of 17 years 37 days in 1964, but the first teenager to break four minutes was Herb Elliott in 1958. There is interest too in the other end of the age range, and Ireland's Eamonn Coghlan attracted world-wide admiration in February 1994 when he became the first veteran (i.e. over 40 years of age) to go under four minutes. His time was 3 min 58.15 sec, with successive quarter mile times of 59.10, 60.34, 59.78 and 58.93 sec. This astounding performance was made on a banked indoor track at Harvard University, Cambridge, Massachusetts, and was therefore not allowed as a Veteran's world record. It stands nevertheless as a barely credible feat in the annals of track running.

By a rare coincidence May 1954 saw another mile-stone event in athletics, the first sub-five-minute mile by a woman. She was Diane Leather. The race was in the Midland Women's meeting at Perry Barr, Birmingham, and the winning time was 4 min 59.6 sec, an unofficial world record. (At that time, there was a view that it was dangerous for women to run such a distance and some countries would not even accept the 800m as an official distance for women.) The time was all the more remarkable because only an hour earlier Miss Leather had set a new British women's 800m record of 2 min 14.1 sec. The present world record time for the women's mile is 4 min 12.56 sec, set by Svetlana Masterkova of Russia in Zurich in 1996. Comparisons are irresistible – see the following details:

	1954	1996	Improvement
Men	3:59.4	3:44.39	15.01 sec (6.27%)
Women	4:59.6	4:12.56	47.04 sec (15.70%)

Since 1954 the improvement in the women's world record has been more than three times greater than that in the men's; even in percentage terms the women's improvement has been two-and-a-half times that of the men! Will a woman ever run inside four minutes?

We must wait and see.

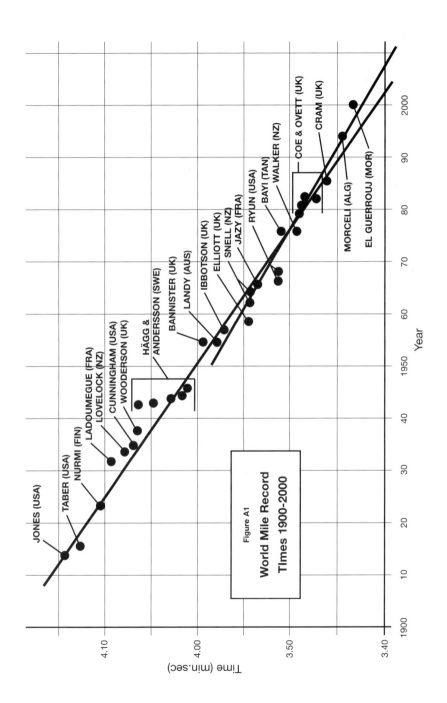

Figure A1

World Mile Record
Times 1900-2000

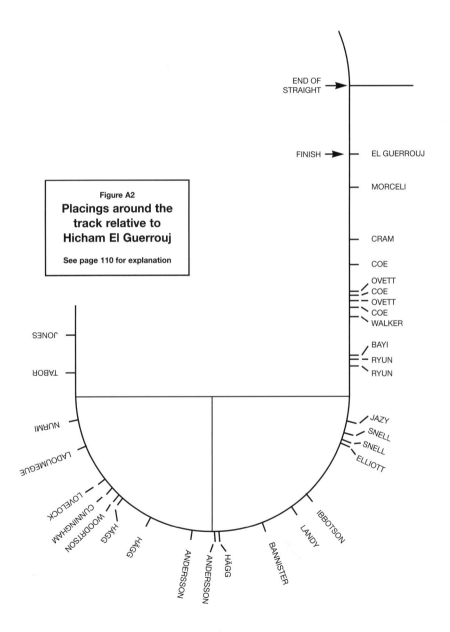

END OF
STRAIGHT →

FINISH → — EL GUERROUJ

— MORCELI

— CRAM

— COE

OVETT
COE
OVETT
COE
WALKER

BAYI
RYUN
RYUN

JONES —

TABOR —

JAZY
SNELL
SNELL
ELLIOTT

NURMI

LADOUMEGUE

LOVELOCK
CUNNINGHAM
WOODRTISON
HÄGG
HÄGG

ANDERSSON

ANDERSSON

HÄGG

BANNISTER

LANDY

IBBOTSON

Figure A2

Placings around the track relative to Hicham El Guerrouj

See page 110 for explanation

Appendix II
A RECORD OF TOM HULATT'S RACES (1949-1960)

Date	Venue	Event	Position	Time	Affiliation
1949					
12 Aug	Tibshelf Sports	880 yds (h)	1st	1 min 58.4 sec	Alfreton LOY
1950					
No details available					
1951					
10 July	?	1 mile (h)	1st	–	Alfreton LOY
July	Riddings Cycle and Athletic Sports	1 mile (h)	1st	4 min 9.4 sec	Alfreton LOY
		880 yds (h)	2nd	–	Alfreton LOY
?	Mansfield Festival Sports, Forest Town	1 mile (h)	1st	4 min 15 sec	Alfreton D LOY
		880 yds (h)	1st	1 min 53.4 sec	Alfreton D LOY
?	Ilkeston Charity Athletic Sports	1 mile (h)	2nd	–	Alfreton & District LOY
		880 yds (h)	2nd	–	Alfreton
10 Aug	Holmewood, Chesterfield	1 mile (h)	1st	–	–
		880 yds (h)	1st	–	
11 Aug	Tibshelf Sports	3 miles (s)	name appeared in programme		Alfreton LOY
		1 mile (h)	1st	–	Alfreton LOY
		880 yds (h)	1st	1 min 58.4 sec	Alfreton LOY
		440 yds (h)	name appeared in programme		Alfreton LOY
28 Aug	NUM Gala	1 mile (h)	name appeared in programme		–
		880 yds (h)	name appeared in programme		
?	B.S.A. Sports Club Meeting, Small Heath	880 yds (s)	2nd	–	Alfreton AC
Sept	Uttoxeter Wakes Sports	880 yds	retired with badly twisted knee		–
1952					
May	Bournville Sports, Birmingham	1 mile (inv)	4th	4 min 17 sec	Alfreton AC
?	Lincoln	880 yds	1st	–	–
7 June	NCAA Championships, Billingham	1 mile	1st * *	4 min 23 sec	Alfreton AC
		880 yds	not placed	–	Alfreton AC
20 June	AAA Championships, White City, London	1 mile	–	–	Alfreton AC
28 June	Municipal Sports, Chesterfield	1 mile (match)	3rd	–	N.C. (Northern Counties)
		1 mile (open)	not placed	–	Airedale Harriers
		880 yds	not placed	–	–

Date	Event / Location	Distance	Placing	Time	Club
July	BSA Silver Trophy, Birmingham	880 yds (s)	2nd	–	–
7 July	Belper Wakes Sports	1 mile	1st *	4 min 20.6 sec	Alfreton AC
?	BR Championships, Loughton, Essex	1 mile	1st	–	Alfreton AC
		880 yds	1st	–	Alfreton AC
Aug	Clay Cross & Danesmoor Sports	1 mile	not placed	–	Alfreton AC
		880 yds (h)	placing not known		Alfreton AC
Aug	Holmewood, Chesterfield	1 mile	1st	–	Alfreton AC
		880 yds	1st	–	Alfreton AC
9 Aug	Tibshelf Sports	1 mile (h)	name appeared in programme	–	Alfreton AC
		880 yds (h)	3rd	–	Alfreton AC
		440 yds (h)	name appeared in programme	–	Alfreton AC
?	Lincoln	1 mile (h. inv)	2nd	–	Alfreton AC
?	Rolls-Royce Welfare Ground, Derby	1 mile (h)	1st	4 min 11.6 sec	Alfreton AC

1953

Date	Event / Location	Distance	Placing	Time	Club
16 May	Staveley I & C Co., Sports Ground	1 mile	1st *	4 min 27.2 sec	Alfreton AC
20 June	NCAA Championships, Hull	1 mile	1st * *	4 min 24.6 sec	–
		880 yds	4th	1 min 58.8 sec	–
27 June	NCAA v. AAU Eire, Chesterfield	1 mile	1st	4 min 18.2 sec	NC
July	AAA Championships, White City, London	1 mile	5th	–	Alfreton AC
8 Aug	Tibshelf Sports	3 miles	name appeared in programme	–	Unattached
		1 mile (h)	placing not known		Unattached
		880 yds (h)	placing not known		Unattached
?	Inter-Club Competition, Clipstone, Mansfield	880 yds	2nd	–	Mansfield
?	Wellington AC Sports	1 mile (h. inv)	2nd	–	Tibshelf

1954

Date	Event / Location	Distance	Placing	Time	Club
Apr	Fallowfield, Manchester	1 mile	1st	4 min 24.9 sec	Derbyshire AAA
6 May	OUAC v. AAA, Oxford	1 mile	3rd	4 min 16.0 sec	Alfreton
May	Municipal Sports, Rotherham	1 mile (inv)	2nd	–	Polytechnic H
?	Bournville Sports, Birmingham	1 mile (s. inv)	2nd	–	Polytechnic H
19 June	NCAA Championships, Manchester	1 mile	not placed	–	Polytechnic H
21 June	Derby & County AC Annual Mtg., Derby	3 miles (s)	1st	14 min 6.2 sec	Polytechnic H
5 July	Belper Wakes Sports	1 mile (s)	2nd	–	Polytechnic H
14 July	Coronation Trophy Sports, Darlington	1 mile (h. inv)	1st	4 min 13 sec	Polytechnic H
2 Aug	Bentinck Welfare Sports	1 mile (h)	3rd	–	Polytechnic H
		880 yds (h)	not placed	–	Polytechnic H

Date	Venue	Distance	Position	Time	Club
7 Aug	Tibshelf Sports	3 miles	2nd	–	Polytechnic H
11 Aug	The Hague, Holland	1500m	1st	3 min 57.4 sec	Polytechnic H
		3000m	1st (equal)	8 min 57.4 sec	Polytechnic H
14 Aug	Leiden, Holland	4 x 1500m relay	Team won	3 min 53.2 sec (personal) 15 min 55.4 sec (team)	Polytechnic H
		3000m	1st (equal)	8 min 44.4 sec	Polytechnic H
Aug	Sports Arena, Croydon	2 miles	1st (equal)	9 min 9.8 sec	Polytechnic H
4 Sept	Markham Collieries Sports	1 mile (h)	name appeared in programme		Polly (sic) H
		880 yds (h)	name appeared in programme		Polly (sic) H
9 Oct	London-Brighton Road Race	August cuttings mention that W.T.H. will be running but there is no information that he actually ran.			
		1955			
?	Whirlow, Sheffield	1 mile	2nd	–	–
		880 yds	2nd	–	Tibshelf
25 June	NCAA Championships, Manchester	3 miles	not placed	–	Tibshelf H and AC
		1 mile	not placed	–	Tibshelf H and AC
?	Rubery Owen Sports, Wrexham	1 mile (inv)	1st	4 min 15.8 sec	Mansfield Harriers
10 Sept	John Players Sports, Nottingham	880 yds (h)	not placed	–	Tibshelf Harriers
		1956			
?	Derbys AAA Champs, Staveley	1 mile	1st *	4 min 17.4 sec	Tibshelf AC
		880 yds	1st *	1 min 56.1 sec	Tibshelf AC
23 June	NCAA Championships, Manchester	1 mile	not placed	–	–
25 Aug	Hillsborough Park, Sheffield	no details of distance or result available			
		1957			
?	Strelley Road Playing Fields, Nottingham	880 yds	1st	1 min 58.9 sec	Sutton-in-Ashfield H
May/Jun	Hillsborough Park, Sheffield	1 mile (inv)	3rd	–	Alfreton
		3000m s.c.	1st	9 min 26.4 sec	–
		1958			
21 June	NCAA Championships, Manchester	3000m s.c.	1st **	9 min 28.6 sec	Alfreton AC and Chesterfield Harriers
?	Police Sports, Ashbrooke, Sunderland	1 mile (h. inv)	3rd	–	Alfreton AC
?	Scunthorpe, Lincs	880 yds (s)	1st	2 min 4.6 sec	Chesterfield Harriers
July	Kinnaird Trophy Meeting, Chiswick	3000m s.c. (inv)	1st	9 min 9.6 sec	Alfreton and Chesterfield H

Date	Event / Venue	Distance	Place	Time	Team
7 July	Sports Ground, Staveley	1 mile	1st *	4 min 15.9 sec	Alfreton AC
		880 yds	not placed	–	Alfreton AC
11/12 July	AAA Championships, White City, London	3000m s.c.	6th	9 min 11.4 sec	Alfreton and Chesterfield Harriers
?	Inter-Club Match, Nottingham	1 mile	1st	4 min 14.0 sec	Alfreton and Chesterfield Harriers
?	Match v. Nigerian Team, Berry Hill, Mansfield	1 mile	1st	4 min 12.4 sec	Notts
		880 yds	3rd	–	–
?	GB v. Empire Match, White City, London	3000m s.c. (inv)	2nd	9 min 9.2 sec	Alfreton and Chesterfield Harriers
14 Aug	Chesterfield H & AC Championships, Chesterfield	1 mile	1st	–	–
		880 yds	1st	–	–
6 Sept	Synthonia v. AAA Match, Billingham	3000m s.c.	3rd	–	Synthonia
1959					
May	Inter-County Championships, White City, London	3000m s.c.	no details available		Hallamshire
20 June	NCAA Championships, Manchester	3000m s.c.	not placed	–	–
3 Aug	Miners' Sports, Berry Hill, Mansfield	1 mile	1st	–	–
Aug	Roundhay Park, Leeds	3 miles (s)	1st	14 min 16.2 sec	Hallamshire
Aug	Inter-Club Match, Rawmarsh, Sheffield	1 mile	1st	4 min 26.0 sec	Hallamshire
20 Aug	Chesterfield H & AC Championships, Chesterfield	1 mile	1st	–	–
		880 yds	1st	–	–
		220 yds	2nd	–	–
?	Harvey Hadden Stadium, Nottingham	3000m s.c.	1st	9 min 42.4 sec	–
1960					
Jan	Derbys. Cross-Country Championships, Kedleston Park, Derby	6 miles	8th	–	Hallamshire
Apr	Club Road Race, Rivelin, Sheffield	5 miles	1st	–	Hallamshire
?	Club Road Race, Rivelin, Sheffield	6½ miles	2nd	34 min 26 sec	Hallamshire
?	NCAA Championships	3000m s.c.	2nd	9 min 28.2 sec	Hallamshire H and AC
6 Aug	Tibshelf Sports	3 miles	3rd	–	Hallamshire
		1 mile	not placed	–	–
?	Inter-Club Match, Headingley, Leeds	2 miles	1st	9 min 25.2 sec	Hallamshire
?	Club Meeting, Sheffield	2 miles	1st	9 min 24.0 sec	Hallamshire
?	Harvey Hadden Stadium, Nottingham	3000m s.c.	1st	10 min 5.0 sec	Hallamshire

Abbreviations: h – handicap, s – scratch, Inv – invitation, s.c. – steeplechase. Note: * Derbyshire County Champion, ** Northern Counties Champion

122

INDEX

*Main references only

A40, 26
Amateur Athletic Association (AAA)
   Championships, 71, 73, 80, 85, 87, 95, 114
   formal invitation, 74
   Records Committee, 34
   selection process, 51, 95
   selectors, 14, 16, 95
   team, 10, 12, 13, 16
   team manager, 20
   vest, 48
Achilles Club, 4, 11, 14, 57
Adcocks, Bill, 5
Alfreton, 12, 41, 43, 44, 45, 49, 62, 68
Alfreton Athletic Club, 41, 42, 43, 48, 70, 72, 73,
   77, 79, 85, 89, 92
Alfreton and Chesterfield Harriers, 85, 86
Alfreton Local Library, 41, 43
Alfreton LOY, 68
All-Ireland Championships (1954), 12
all-weather surface, 19
amusements, 63
Anderson, Arne, 102, 103, 108
announcer, 20
Archer, Jeffrey, 37
Army, 46, 48, 51, 65, 66, 68
athletic immortality, 30

Babbington Colliery Co Ltd, 62
Babbington Street, 50, 52, 90, 91
Bailey, McDonald, 72
Baillie, W, 40
Bannister, RG*, 3, 9, 13, 22, 34, 38, 39, 54, 79,
   104, 105, 109
Bannister Close, 58
barrack damages, 66
barrier, 108, 109
Bates, J, 5
Bayi, Filbert, 102, 103
BBC, 27, 96
BBC television newsreel, 28

Beamon, Bob, 108
Belfry, The, 60
Belper Wakes Sports, Derbyshire, 71, 80
Bentinck Colliery, 68, 80
Beresford, Mike, 84
Berry Hill Ground, Mansfield, 86, 88
Bess of Hardwick, 94
best fit, 107
Billingham on Tees, Durham, 70, 80, 86
Blue Bell Inn, 46
Boat Race, 111
Bolsover, Derbyshire, 16, 44, 54
Bolsover Castle, 51, 54
Bournville Sports, Birmingham, 70
Boyd, I, 40
Brasher, CW*, 3, 11, 15, 25, 28, 35, 55, 74, 84, 99
Breckinridge, A, 17
British All-comers record, 15, 18, 22, 35
British Amateur Athletic Board (BAAB),
   20, 30, 35, 81, 113
British Athletics Federation, 98
British Empire Record, 22, 38
British Games, 84
British Gaumont, 28
British Mile Champion, 74
British National Record, 14, 15, 18, 22, 35
BSA Silver Trophy, Small Heath, Birmingham, 71
BSA Sports club, Small Heath, Birmingham, 69
Bullivant, Michael, 87
Burghley, Lord, 72
buying out, 66

Cambridge Alumni Magazine (CAM), 6, 25
Cambridge Biographical Encyclopedia, 36
Cannell, Robert, 28
Cape Town, 50, 64, 78
Catterick Camp, Yorkshire, 65
celebrations, 27, 76, 78
champagne, 27
channel swimmers, 49
Chataway, CJ*, 3, 11, 15, 28, 29, 35, 37, 74, 99
Chataway's car, 26, 28

Chelsea Barracks, 14, 21
Cheshire County team, 74
Chesterfield, Derbyshire, 16, 45, 62, 71
Chesterfield Harriers and Athletic Club,
  16, 77, 85, 86, 88, 89, 92
Chesterfield Hospital, 91, 93
Christie AC, Manchester, 74
Church Lane, 49, 61, 64, 66, 82, 89
cinder track, 19, 72, 112
Clarke, Anne, 5
Clarke, Ron, 114
'clash of the giants', 38
Clipstone, Mansfield, 73
coal mining, 12, 62
Coe, Sebastian, 102, 103, 106
Coghlan, Eamonn, 114
collieries (pits)
  Grassmoor, 62
  Holmewood, 62, 66, 67, 79
  Pilsley, 62
  Tibshelf, 62
  Williamthorpe, 62, 66, 67, 77, 78, 92
comfrey, 67
concessionary coal, 63
Coronation Trophy Sports, Darlington, 80
county archives, 57
Cram, Steve, 102, 103, 108
Croft, Colin, 4, 46, 49, 67
crosswind, 33
Crown, The, 45
Croydon Sports Arena, 81
Crump, J, 15, 20, 24, 30, 31, 34, 35, 81, 113
Cunningham, Glen, 102

Daley, Arthur, 31
De'ath, John, 4, 11, 36, 41, 57, 58, 59, 60
Derby and County Athletic Club, 4, 12, 80, 84
Derby Local studies library, 41
Derby Locomotive Works, 12
Derbyshire, 3, 12, 16
Derbyshire Amateur Athletic Association (DAAA),
  4, 56, 61, 68, 71, 72, 74, 83, 92, 98
Derbyshire County Council, 62
Derbyshire County One-Mile Champion,

71, 72, 73, 76, 80, 82, 85, 92
Derbyshire longhouse, 45
Derwent Valley, 41
Dimmock, Peter, 26, 78
Disley, John, 85
Dodsworth, Richard, 57
dogs and pets, 52
Dole, GF*, 10, 17, 18, 19, 54, 78
double rainbow, 33
Dream Mile, 31
Dunkley, 81
Dutch all-comers record, 81
Dyson, Geoff, 19

Egyptian Army mile record, 16, 77
Ekkehand zur Megede, 22
Eldon, Stan, 87
El Guerrouj, Hicham, 58, 102, 103, 109, 110, 111
Elliot, Herb, 89, 102, 103, 105, 110, 114
embrocation, 67
Empire and Commonwealth Games
  1954 – Vancouver, 9, 17, 37, 38, 39, 40
  1958 – Cardiff, 84, 85, 86
Empire Team, 86
Emsley Carr Mile, 13, 86
English Nature Record, 22, 35
engrossments, 64
European Games
  1954 – Berne, 9, 17
  1958 – Stockholm, 84, 85, 86
European Record, 22
Evans, 81
Everest, 3
Everett, Graham, 86
examinations, 33
Exeter College, Oxford, 22

fallibility of the press, 46
Fallowfield, Manchester, 53, 74, 77, 79
Fenners Cambridge, 19
Ferguson, R, 40
fifteen-hundred metres (1500m),
  9, 23, 37, 38, 93, 108
Finland, 37

First Four Minutes, 9
Five Pits Trail, 43, 48, 62
five thousand metres (5000m), 28
foot and mouth outbreak, 48, 49
Fort Knox, 56
four-minute mile*, 3, 15, 21, 31, 48, 75, 111
four-minute mile (40th anniversary celebrations)
　36, 44, 48, 58, 59, 97, 98, 99
Fox, Paul, 27
Freshman's mile record, 16, 77
full blue, 26

garden produce, 63
Geddes, Andrew, 93
George, Walter, 101
Glover, Eric, 5, 52
Gordon, AD*, 10, 17, 24, 44, 53, 76, 85
Gordon, Dr JD, 44, 54, 75
Great Britain team, 86
Great Britain v Empire, 87
Guiness Book of Athletics Facts and Feats (The), 25
Guiness Book of Records (The), 20

Hackett, Desmond, 33
Hägg, Gundar, 23, 31, 102, 103, 108
Halberg, Murray, 17, 40, 86
handicap events, 69, 85
Hardwick Hall, 51
Hardwick Hall six mile road race, 48, 49, 93
Hardy, Eddie, 71, 80, 92
Harrow on the Hill, 26
Harvey Hadden Stadium, Nottingham, 88, 89
Hayes Trophy, 88
heading and tailing, 52
Heath, 65, 72
Hechtel Stadium, Belgium, 113
Hertford College, Oxford, 93
Herriott, Maurice, 86, 87
Hesketh, G Everard, 5, 51, 52, 90, 91, 99
Hewson, Brian, 85
Hill, Cecil, 4, 45, 46, 68
Hill, Margaret, 4, 45, 46
Hillary, Edmund, 3
Hillsborough football ground, Sheffield, 59

Hillsborough Park Sports Arena, Sheffield, 83, 84
"History Man, The", 36
Holland, (1954), 48, 81, 82
Holmewood Sports, Chesterfield 69, 71
horseshoes, 52
Hulatt, Ann, 3, 5, 11, 45, 46, 47, 48, 49, 50, 51,
　61, 64, 65, 77, 78, 89, 90, 92, 98
Hulatt, Annette, 47, 64, 75
Hulatt, Annie, 47, 61, 75, 78, 79, 90, 91, 98
Hulatt, CH (Harry), 46, 61, 90, 98
Hulatt, Harry, 47, 50, 64, 65, 75, 76, 78
Hulatt, Vernon, 64
Hulatt, WT (Tom)
　AAA team member, 3, 10, 11, 12, 14, 23, 24, 95
　affiliations, see appendix II
　authors' early contact, 10, 11, 12, 41-50, 53
　best man, 52, 90
　coaching, 16, 88, 90
　cross country/road running, 88
　Derbyshire County Champion, 56, 71, 72
　early days, 56, 62-73
　family, 52, 61, 62, 64, 65, 66, 90, 91
　Field Captain, 72
　hobbies, 90, 91, 96
　memorial, 93, 94
　military service, 65, see also Army
　motivation, 67, 80, 84, 85, 86
　Northern Counties Champion, 16, 70, 72
　obituaries, 6, 42, 44, 91, 94
　Pest Control Office, 90, 91, 92
　running career, see Appendix II
　schools, 62, 65
　Tom's recollections, 44, 75, 76, 96, 97
　training, 67, 71, 74, 77, 79, 82, 89
　venues, see Appendix II
Hunt, Dr, 49
Hunt, Freda, 42, 43, 44
Hunter, Linda, 4

Ibbotson, Derek, 84, 86, 102, 109
Iffley Road*, 3, 18, 19, 36, 57, 59, 93, 112
Ilkeston Charity Athletic Sports, 69
International Association of Athletics Federations -
　previously International Amateur Athletic Federation

(IAAF)
  22, 23, 25, 34, 35, 101
Jack Russells, 90
Jackdaw Lane, 58
Jackson, Denise, 5
Jackson, Stephanie, 5
Jazy, Michel, 102
Johansson, Denis, 39
Jones, John Paul, 101, 102, 103

Kallio, Aulis, 39
Kedleston Park, Derby, 88
Keily, Arthur, 4, 12, 41, 56, 87, 98
Keily, Joe, 4, 56
Keino, Kipchoge, 58
Kelly Cup, 86, 88
Kinnaird Trophy, 85, 86
Komen, Daniel, 113
Kuts, Vladimir, 10, 28

Ladoumégue, Jules, 102
Landy, JM,
  9, 13, 17, 32, 33, 36, 37, 38, 39, 40, 48, 71,
  81, 93, 102, 105, 108, 110
  lap timings, 23
  Law, DC, 14, 40
Lawrence, DH, 62
Lawrence, Frances, 4
League of Youth (LOY), 57, 68
Leason, Cyril,
  4, 5, 43, 44, 46, 47, 48, 49, 50, 51, 65, 67, 72,
  78, 89, 90, 92, 93
Leason, Eric, 49, 90
Leather, Diane, 114
Leeson, Christine, 4, 44
Lime Grove Studios, London, 26, 27, 78
Livesey, George, 5, 57, 111
local study centres, 57
London to Brighton road race, 81
London v Moscow, 1954, 28
Lovelock, Jack, 102
Lueg, Werner, 23

Mackay, Duncan, 36

Madan Mohan, Kay, 27
Manchester Central Library, 44
Mansfield, 73
Mansfield Festival Sports, Forest Town, 69
Mansfield Harriers, Appendix II
marathon, 12,38,98
Markham Collieries Sports, 81
Masterkova, Svetlana, 114
match programme,
  11, 14, 20, 36, 43, 47, 50, 53, 57, 78, 79
Matlock, 62
Matthews, Peter, 25
McGoverne, T, 88
McWhirter, Norris, 20, 22
McWhirter, Ross, 20
media, 28
media coverage, 10
memorabilia, 36, 57, 59
memorial stone, 43, 46, 48, 49
Merton College, Oxford, 22
Metcalf, Jack, 87
Miller, TN, 4, 11, 16, 17, 18, 24, 53, 98, 99
Milligan, V, 40
miner, 65, 66, 95
mining community, 63
Miracle Mile, The, 29, 37
Moor, R, 20
Morceli, Noureddine, 102, 106
Motspur Park, 15, 17, 19, 35
Mugglestone, Simon, 59, 93, 106

Nankeville, W (Bill), 19
National Centre for Athletic Literature (NCAL),
  5, 56, 57, 112
National Playing Fields Association (NPFA),
  5, 19, 57, 112
National Service, 16, 65, 66
National Trust, 94
Newspapers
  Chad, 6, 42, 43, 44, 46, 91
  Croydon Advertiser, 6,
  Croydon Times, 81
  Daily Express,
  5, 18, 25, 26, 27, 28, 33, 35, 95, 96, 97, 106

Daily Herald, 5, 26, 31, 32, 35, 113
Daily Mail, 33
Daily Mirror, 5, 25, 31, 32, 105, 109
Daily Sketch, 5, 25, 27, 31, 35
Daily Telegraph, 5, 14, 15, 18, 20, 24, 25,
30,34, 35, 46, 99, 113
Derby Evening Telegraph, 6, 44, 78, 97, 98, 100
Derbyshire Times, 6, 42, 44, 53, 75, 77
Echo, 42, 43, 48
Guardian Journal, 23, 31
Independent, 93
News Chronicle, 20, 25, 31, 32, 105
Sheffield Telegraph, 83
Sunday Express, 96
Sunday Times, 5, 20, 21, 28
The Times,
5, 15, 17, 24, 25, 28, 29, 32, 35, 36, 93, 106
Nigerian Team, 86, 92
Norman, Percy, 42, 51, 69, 70, 71, 72, 73
Northern Counties Athletic Association (NCAA),
4, 16, 51, 56, 61, 68, 72, 73, 80
Northern Counties Championships,
12, 70, 80, 83, 84, 86, 92
Northern Counties One-Mile Champion,
16, 70, 71, 72, 73, 76, 87
notice (request for information), 43, 44, 46
Nottingham Athletic Club, 88
Nottingham Track Association, 88
Nottinghamshire AAA, 86
Notts and Derbys coal field, 61
NUM gala, 69
Nurmi, Paavo, 102, 103, 108, 110

Oaten, HJ, 32
O'Connor, T, 33
Old Ale House, The, 58
Olympics Games,
1928, Amsterdam, 72
1948, London, 9, 72
1952, Helsinki, 9, 25, 37, 71, 74
1956, Melbourne, 10, 84
1960, Rome, 108
1968, Mexico City, 108
2008, Beijing, 104

Olympic Park, Melbourne, 13
Ovett, Steve, 102, 103, 110
OUAC v AAA match
1953, 15
1954, 4, 14, 18, 34, 35, 47, 74, 75
Oxford v Cambridge match, 16, 54, 93
Oxford Olympians, 59
Oxford University Alumni office, 16, 53
Oxford University Athletic Club (OUAC)
club, 10, 20, 53, 57
honorary secretary, 16, 17
president, 16, 17, 19
team, 16, 17, 53
Oxford University sports complex, 10, 57, 58
oxygen intake, 34

pace maker/making, 14, 25, 35, 36
parents' priorities, 63
Parker, B, 5
pay, 67
Peak District, The, 62
Pembroke College, Oxford, 9, 93
Penn, A, 5
Pennington, R, 18
Peters, Jim, 38
Piccadilly Circus, 28
Pilsley, 43, 45, 47, 48, 65, 78, 93
Pincher, Chapman, 34
Pirie, Gordon, 13, 17, 81, 84, 87
pits, see 'collieries'
placingo, 55
platelayer, 65, 72
Polytechnic Harriers, Chiswick, 44, 81, 82, 92
press-cuttings, 41, 48, 56, 67, 68, 69, 71, 73, 83, 89
"Progression of World Best Performances and
Official IAAF World Records", 22, 39
Proctor, David, 112
psychological battle, 38
public transport, 63

Queen's Birthday Honours, 99
Queens College, Cambridge, 55
Queens Coronation, 3, 28
Queen's Ground, Chesterfield, 73

race number cards, 47, 50
ratification, 34 et seq
ratification criterion, 35
ratting, 52, 90
Rawmarsh, Sheffield, 88
Riddings Cycle and Athletic Sports, 69
Rivelin, Sheffield, 88
Roberts, Bryn, 5, 27, 57, 111
Rolls Royce Welfare Ground, Derby, 71
Roston, Frank, 34
Rotherham Municipal Sports, 80
Roundhay Park, Leeds, 88
Royal Air Force, 66
Royal Court Theatre, Sloane Square, 27
Royal Electrical and Mechanical Engineers, 65
Royal Navy, 66
Royal Oak, 45
Runners World, 4, 24, 25, 36, 53, 98
Ryun, Jim, 93, 102, 103, 108, 114

Santee, Wes, 13, 15, 17, 32, 37, 108
Schofield, 81
Scott, Steve, 93
scrapbooks, 48, 49, 50, 61, 67, 73
scratch, 80
scrutineers, 36
Scunthorpe, Lincs, 85
Second World War, 3, 21, 62, 64, 108
Selston, 42, 43, 89
shandy, 26, 46
Shaw, Dave, 87
Sherwood Forest, 62
Shirley, Eric, 85
Skegness, 52
Snell, Peter, 102, 103
sound barrier, 31
South Africa, 47, 50, 53, 64, 66, 76
South African Air Force, 50, 64, 76
Spedding, R 4
sponsorship, 103
Sportsman's Book Club, 9
"Sportsview", 26, 27, 78
Stacey, Nicholas, 25
Stampfl, Franz, 14, 20, 21, 23, 25

starter, 20
starter's pistol, 36, 59, 111
Staveley Iron and Chemical Co. Ground, Staveley,
    72
Strand, Lennart, 23
steeplechase (3000m), 56, 84, 85, 86, 87, 88, 89,
    92
St George's flag, 21, 36, 59
St John's church, 19, 21, 33, 36, 58, 59
Stocks, Margaret, 4, 42, 43, 68, 73, 89
stopwatches, 37, 59, 111
Strelley Road Playing Fields, Notts, 83
Sunderland Police Sports Ground, 85
Surrey schools sports, 1953, 15
Susan, 58
Sutton in Ashfield Harriers, 84

Tabor, Norman, 102, 103, 108
Taipale, Ilmari, 39
Tenzing, Norgay, 3
Territorial Army, 66
Tibshelf AC, 83
Tibshelf schools, 62, 65
Tibshelf Show, 45, 67, 68, 69, 71, 73, 80, 89, 92
timekeepers, 20, 29, 34, 111
Tom Hullatt Trophy, 94
track layout, 109, 110, 111, 112
Trelford, Donald, 14, 25, 46, 99
Truelove, LR, 20, 25
Tulloh, Bruce, 36
Turku, Finland, 37, 48, 71

UK all-time mile list, 17
Universities Athletic Union, 86
University College, Oxford, Development Office,
    16, 53, 55
University Sports Ground, Hull, 72
University Sports Ground, Nottingham, 85
Uttoxeter Wakes Sports, 70

Villanova University, 17
Vincent's Club, Oxford, 26, 46
Vuorisalo, Olavi, 39

Walker, John, 93, 102, 105
Walker, D, 80
wall plaque, 48, 65
Watts, T, 4, 44, 46
Welsh AAA, 83
Welsh Universities, 55
Wembley Stadium, 20
Wenger, Jean, 5, 112
Westwoods, 45, 49, 50, 52, 61, 66, 82, 90
White City Stadium, London,
    10, 16, 28, 71, 73, 77, 84, 85, 93, 114
White City Stadium, Manchester, 56, 83
White Smith, Percy, 19, 112
Whirlow, Sheffield, 82, 83
Whitfield, Mel, 17
Whitman, Slim, 90
Wilkinson, Peter, 5, 87, 88
Willcox, PDT, 4, 11, 57
Williams, Sue, 100
Wilson, Douglas, 73
Wilson, Peter, 109
Wood, Ken, 80, 83, 84
wood yard, 65
Wooderson, Sidney, 17, 102, 105
World Record, 22, 37, 38, 101

Also available from the publishers of *The First Four-Minute Mile* and *Tom Hulatt of Tibshelf*

FUNNY RUNNING SHORTS
101 true stories from the world of running
by Geoff Wightman and Dave Bedford

THE PERFECT GIFT FOR ANY RUNNER  **£9.99**

Do you know ...

- What went disastrously wrong in Peter Elliott's first cross-country race?
- What did Zola Budd say the moment she heard she had been granted British citizenship?
- Why did Seb Coe nearly get sent home from the European Championships as a disciplinary measure?
- Why did Nick Rose have to be back in Britain the morning after winning the masters New York Marathon title?
- Who set a road relay lap record wearing a bat cape?
- What did Paula Radcliffe dream about the night before winning the Flora London Marathon?
- Who tried to roll to the finish of a major marathon?
- Who travelled all the way to Los Angeles for a 10k road race only to get run over by a wheelchair? Who returned from a four hour run on the back of a fire engine?
- Who on earth would take a ferret for a walk?
- How do portaloos fly?

It's all there in this brand new book of running humour, compiled by two veterans of the UK running scene and published by Descartes, the company that brings you *Athletics Weekly* magazine.

United Kingdom £9.99 (plus 50p p&p).
Available from Descartes Publishing Limited, 83 Park Road, Peterborough. PE1 2TN. Tel: 01733-343457

Mile